HONORING the American Past

The Stories of America's World War II Veterans

PEARSON

Prentice Hall

Needham, Massachusetts
Upper Saddle River, New Jersey
Glenview, Illinois

This guide was made possible in part through the generosity of Mr. Frank DeCicco who was a member of the Eighth Air Force, 303rd Bomb Group, and the entire DeCicco family, Mrs. Jean DeCicco and their daughters, Jessica, Deborah, Rebecca, Mary Angela and Ellie.

Cover: The crew of the B-17 Flying Fortress *Knock-out Dropper* walk away from their plane on Norvember 17, 1943.

ISBN 0-13-181499-0

1 2 3 4 5 6 7 8 9 10 07 06 05 04 03

Table of Contents

Introduction

By Craig Harris, President of the Eighth Air Force Historical Society

Today's United States Air Force, with global capability for defending freedom and protecting our nation, is just over a half-century old. Born of necessity and fought for by Americans of great vision, it was forged in the crucible of two world wars, barely surviving the obstacles placed in its course during the years between.

The United States Army Air Forces

When the United States entered World War I in 1917, it was virtually without a combat air force. It had only the 1914 U.S. Army Aviation Section (Signal Corps), a successor to the Aeronautical Section of the Signal Corps (1907). Few in the United States had seen any role for aircraft beyond observation and reconnaissance. After the Wright Brothers made the first powered aircraft flight in 1903, it was the European powers that turned the airplane into an instrument of war.

The outbreak of World War I in 1914 found Great Britain, France, and Germany with primitive air forces that, with the imperative of war, evolved rapidly in quantity and combat effectiveness. By 1918, when the newly named United States Army Air Service sent its first flyers into combat in British and French aircraft, European combatants were engaged in air-to-air combat and bombing of enemy positions in addition to scouting functions. By the end of the war the United States was on its way to developing an air arm and American airmen had given good accounts of themselves. The impact of American manufacturing might was beginning to be felt.

After World War I many people who had become aware of the potential of the airplane as a weapon departed France with the belief that the next war would be waged in the air. However, in the United States the years following the war saw a retrenchment in military strength, emphasizing economy and conventional weapons. The fledgling Army Air Service had to make do with obsolete aircraft left over from the war. Although the Army Air Service continued to push for more air capability their efforts were impeded by rivalries among the armed services. General William Mitchell, who had led a major raid on German positions in 1918, fought so hard with the War Department for increased air power that he angered his superiors, faced court-martial, and was suspended from duty. Before he was suspended he convinced the military that airplanes armed with bombs could destroy obsolete warships. Mitchell resigned from the Army but continued the fight for air power. In large part many of his predictions about the role of air power later came to pass because of his efforts.

In 1926 the Army Air Corps became the army branch for aviation, raising it to the same organizational level as the Infantry, Artillery, and the Quartermaster Corps. The next year Charles A. Lindbergh's solo flight from New York to Paris captured the nation's imagination. Aviation expanded its role in American society in both civilian activities and the military. The American public thrilled to air shows and air races. Many young men and women who would later serve as military flyers became air enthusiasts at air shows, watching "barnstorming" pilots.

New development of bombing and pursuit (fighter) aircraft began and accelerated through the 1930s. The Navy dropped its objections to the Army's Air Service once it received permission to organize its own fleet of airplanes and add several aircraft carriers to the fleet. Army and Navy aviation were beginning to come of age at the end of the decade. By the start of World War II Great Britain, Japan and the United States counted on the aircraft carrier to give them control of the air over the sea.

In 1941 the approach of war made the military planners aware of the need for stronger army aviation. As a result, they created the Army Air Forces (AAF) in June just six months before war came to the United States with the surprise Japanese attack on naval ships and installations at our main Pacific military base at Pearl Harbor in the Hawaiian Islands. The AAF, suddenly thrust into war, grew rapidly in personnel and aircraft. Young men volunteered for service in great numbers and development and production of existing aircraft designs were accelerated. The Army Air Forces achieved a form of independence in early 1942 when it was raised to equal command with Army Ground Forces. Nevertheless, these two units remained within the Army's command structure.

The Eighth Air Force

This is the story of the Eighth Air Force, activated in Savannah, Georgia on January 28, 1942—only seven weeks after the December 7, 1941 attack on Pearl Harbor. The military decided in those early months that the Eighth would go to England and become the primary strategic air force. That is to say, it would be responsible for the destruction of Germany's ability to manufacture and distribute materials such as munitions, fuel, airplanes and tanks necessary to wage war. *Strategic bombing,* in which bombers targeted an enemy's power to carry out a war, was distinct from later missions of *tactical bombing,* in which air power was used as part of specific battles in cooperation with other branches of the military. By August 1942 the Eighth had flown its first mission with its own aircraft against the enemy.

Young men in their late teens and early twenties came together, trained as fighter pilots, bomber pilots, navigators, bombardiers, and gunners with additional jobs as radio operators and flight engineers, to form the largest single military unit of the war. Young men enlisted out of college, from small towns and big cities and off farms. These citizen-soldiers would become the most formidable air-fighting force ever seen. Others, from all walks of life, would become mechanics, radio specialists, armorers, bomb-loaders, refuelers, parachute-packers, working in all of the ground jobs needed to make it possible to put the airmen into combat. Some had been drafted, but combat air crew service was all voluntary.

"The world had never seen anything like it . . . the Eighth Air Force . . . capable of putting two thousand airplanes over Germany, two thousand planes in a single day. . . . " These were boys who quickly grew to be men, who fought in bitter cold and clouds and took the war to the enemy, and who who were shot down and became prisoners, who died in action or who were fortunate to have survived. These men made an essential contribution to winning the war. They fought because they wanted to stop the killing. The way to stop the killing was to stop the war. And they gave their best to win it.

The Eighth Air Force went on to carry out its mission with the services of 350,000 men and women, of whom about 225,000 saw combat in the air. There were 26,000 killed or missing in action, while 28,000 became prisoners of war. The Eighth was one of the largest units of our military, and suffered the highest casualty rates of any combat unit. History tells us that the Eighth carried out its mission and caused such damage to the enemy that it materially contributed to the collapse of the German Reich in 1945.

The Eighth Air Force was never turned back from a target by enemy action.

We have an abundance of knowledge of the operations of the Eighth Air Force during this pivotal time in history. Official records have been the source for many researchers including Roger A. Freeman of Mays Barn, Essex, England. As a teenager Freeman watched the skies over England filled with roaring aircraft and dubbed the Eighth Air Force "The Mighty Eighth." His books are a prime source of factual information about people, equipment, organization and operational details. Operating from bases in England the Eighth Air Force was accessible to the military and civilian press and visible to neighbors. The daily *Stars and Stripes* and the weekly *Yank* told the world of all that happened, at the time it happened, in the European theater.

But it is from the men of the Eighth, the men who lived the history, that much of our story comes. We have stories from the men themselves, as the lifestyle allowed the writing of diaries and keeping of memoirs. Unlike soldiers in the field whose notes could be captured by the enemy, airmen could leave their writings safely "at home" when they flew combat missions.

Over 195,000 air combat veterans, including liberated prisoners of war, survived the war and their stories are rich with personal history, stories of patriotism, courage, and determination. There are recollections of bravery and fear, skill and mishap, good fortune and bad luck, joy and sorrow, rejoicing and pathos, the agony of prison and forced marches, and the joy of liberation. The veterans of the Eighth Air Force brought these stories home, along with the character values they had developed, and took their place in "the Greatest Generation."

This is their story.

The United States Air Force

On September 18, 1947, the United States Army Air Forces became the independent United States Air Force. Jet propulsion of aircraft debuted even before the end of the war and has been in almost exclusive use since the late 1950s. Soon after the war, new technology broke the sound barrier and brought flights into near-space. The Cold War supported rapid development of aircraft. The United States Air Force played an increasingly central role in all conflicts, beginning with the Berlin Airlift in 1948–1949, through Korea and the Cold War, in Vietnam, Desert Storm, Kosovo, and Afghanistan. The Eighth Air Force, long a part of the Strategic Air Command, participated in all our wars and conflicts and today is the chief weapon for causing deterrent damage to enemies of our nation.

Learn now, the price of freedom.

The Mighty Eighth Air Force Heritage Museum

In 1983, Major General Lewis E. Lyle, USAF Retired, a B-17 veteran of 70 combat missions during World War II, joined with other veterans to begin planning a museum. This museum would honor the men and women who helped defeat Nazi aggression by serving in or supporting the greatest air armada the world had ever seen—the Eighth Air Force. These individuals pledged themselves to honor the courage and commitment of more than 350,000 members of the Eighth Air Force.

Museum planners traveled throughout the United States and Europe, visiting museums and talking with staff from these institutions. The very best elements found among these facilities were then combined to create a dramatic 90,000 square foot museum complex.

On May 14, 1996, to the applause of 5,000 Eighth Air Force veterans, their families, dignitaries, and supporters, the vision became a reality. That date witnessed the dedication of the Mighty Eighth Air Force Heritage Museum in Pooler, Georgia, just west of Savannah.

A tour of the Mighty Eighth Air Force Heritage Museum begins with the story of World War II from Hitler's rise to power through the Battle of Britain and the surprise attack on Pearl Harbor. Further exhibits introduce the Eighth Air Force, and The Mission Experience immerses visitors in the sights and sounds of an Eighth Air Force bomber crew's harrowing flight over Nazi Germany.

The Combat Gallery at the Museum brings enemy aircraft face-to-face with those of the Eighth Air Force. Visitors are able to visually compare the size and structures of combat planes and trainers. Other exhibits include artifacts from downed pilots who escaped from occupied Europe and a reconstructed POW bunk illustrating conditions for those who were captured. The concluding galleries present the story of American air power up until the present day.

The Museum has several different tours and programs available to match the educational needs of various groups. In this way, the classroom teacher partners with our educational staff so that both student and teacher may participate in a total museum experience.

The Mighty Eighth Air Force Heritage Museum is proud to sponsor a **Character Education** program for students. We use concrete examples—artifacts, photographs, and stories from our collections—to illustrate 27 key character values. The museum is a significant place for students to learn teamwork and cooperation, to observe the value of democracy as opposed to totalitarianism, and to witness examples of selfless courage to help others. Illustrations of key character values are included throughout this book.

For more information about the museum, contact:

The Mighty Eighth Air Force Heritage Museum
P.O. Box 1992
Savannah, GA 31402
912-748-8888
912-748-0209 FAX
www.mightyeighth.org

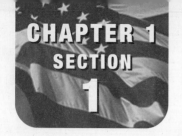

World War I

The Great War

At the dawn of the twentieth century, humans conquered the skies. They learned to fly airplanes. Soon a new breed of warriors—pilots of airplanes that could drop bombs and fire machine guns—were doing battle in the skies over Europe.

Aircraft made their first major military contribution in the "Great War," later known as World War I. Warplanes with names like the "Sopwith Camel" and pilots such as the Red Baron and Eddie Rickenbacker captured the world's attention and became legends. Throughout two world wars and to the present day, air warfare would grow more powerful, more sophisticated, and more dominant in the science of war.

European Alliances

World War I began when the assassination of Archduke Franz Ferdinand of Austria-Hungary on June 28, 1914 triggered a series of events leading to multi-national war. At the start, Germany aligned with its ally, Austria-Hungary. These *Central Powers,* as they were known, were later joined by Bulgaria and the Ottoman Empire.

Opposing the Central Powers were France, Russia, and Britain, and later Italy, known as the *Allies*. Other European nations managed to remain neutral, favoring neither side throughout the war.

Among young gentlemen of Europe, the romantic idea of dashing off to war had become fashionable. Past wars in Europe had been conducted like a gentleman's board game, with armies meeting each other across open fields and playing by certain accepted rules of warfare. World War I and its new technology would change the rules forever.

Confident soldiers on both sides went off to war certain that they would be "home by Christmas," but most would spend more than one Christmas on the battlefield. Many thousands of others would never return home for the holidays.

French soldiers attack from the trenches.

War in the Trenches

For three years, the war remained in a *stalemate*, a situation in which neither side is able to win. The war was worst in France, where both sides threw millions of men into front line battles with little success.

Outdated tactics of sending soldiers charging across an open battlefield led to massive numbers of deaths with no gain of territory. For protection, each side began to dig complex systems of trenches and underground tunnels. Shielded by barbed wire, the trenches protected soldiers from attack, but they also bred rats and disease. Occasionally troops jumped up from the trenches and attacked enemy trenches to gain some ground. Yet most of the attackers, on both sides, were either pushed back or mowed down by enemy gunfire. For much of the war, the front lines hardly budged. The Central Powers and Allies searched for new weapons to break the stalemate and gain the advantage.

As years passed with no breakthrough, most Europeans lost their enthusiasm for the Great War. With families grieving the loss of their men, people going hungry, and countries on the brink of economic collapse, protests against the war flared up. To try to break the stalemate and end the war, both sides competed to bring new, more deadly technology to the battlefield and to the skies.

New Technologies

Many new military technologies debuted after 1914. Rapid-firing *machine guns* dominated the battlefield almost from the start of World War I and accounted for huge numbers of casualties. Exploding *artillery shells* could be launched at targets about 10 miles away. In 1915, Germany introduced one of the greatest horrors of the war, *poison gas*. Fired into the trenches, the gas left soldiers blind, burned, and gasping for air. In 1916, Britain introduced the *armored tank*, designed to break through enemy lines. In later wars, the tank would become a major battlefield warrior, but these early, clumsy versions broke down often and did not make a major contribution until the last days of the war.

Another innovation failed to break the stalemate, but it held great promise for the future: *flying machines*.

The Dirigible

The first aerial vehicle, the hot-air balloon, took to the skies in 1783. Unlike airplanes, which are heavier than air, balloons relied on a sack of lighter-than-air gases—heated air, hydrogen, or helium—to balance the balloonist's weight and lift off the ground.

Inventors made improvements and variations on the balloon, one of which was the dirigible. From the French term *ballon dirigeable*, or "steerable balloon," the dirigible had a rigid frame that made the balloon conform to a certain size and shape. It also became known as the Zeppelin, after its inventor, Count Ferdinand von Zeppelin. The retired German army officer unveiled his variation on the airship in 1910.

Dirigibles at War

These new eyes in the skies drew the attention of military planners, who quickly put balloons and dirigibles into service in World War I. Germany used dirigibles as offensive weapons on both the eastern and western fronts in the war, dropping bombs from the air. Other countries, including the United States, used various types of the lighter-than-air machines for defensive purposes. From high in the air, the Allies observed enemy troop movements, watched for German submarines, provided protection for ships, conducted rescues, and took photographs of enemy positions.

Still, the balloons were slow, hard to steer, and risky to fly. A better flying and fighting machine was on the way.

Science Link | Up, Up, and . . . Where?

Count von Zeppelin's basic concept was a metal frame shaping a giant balloon filled with hydrogen gas. Hydrogen is the lightest known element, and hydrogen gas is lighter than air itself, but highly flammable. Zeppelin's invention had a metal frame inside the balloon, stretching it into the shape of a cylinder with rounded ends; the structure was then covered by fabric.

A hydrogen-filled airship could lift you up, up, up—but how do you make it go somewhere? To navigate, inventors added rudders, flapping wings, paddles, and other oddities, but the best method was found to be a propeller driven by a steam engine and later, a gasoline engine. Zeppelin's first dirigible was 420-feet (128 meters) long, with a 16-horsepower engine connected to two propellers for forward movement. It reached a lumbering speed of 20 miles an hour (32 kilometers an hour).

The golden age of the airship ended in 1937 with the famous, fiery crash of the *Hindenburg,* an 804-foot, hydrogen-filled dirigible, as it attempted to land in New Jersey. Thirty-six people aboard died as horrified Americans listened to coverage of the event on the radio. After the disaster, dirigibles replaced hydrogen gas with helium gas, which is slightly heavier but safe from fire. Nevertheless, the future of lighter-than-air transport was sealed by the crash of the *Hindenburg,* and attention focused instead on airplane technology.

Question: What technological advantages does the airplane have over the dirigible?

The First Airplanes

At the start, the airplane was an exotic oddity. Experts on both sides of the Atlantic Ocean were amazed at the news that two bicycle repairmen from Ohio had mastered one of humankind's greatest achievements: powered flight. The first flight, near Kitty Hawk, North Carolina, on December 17, 1903, was seen by some as a stunt or a hoax. Ignoring the doubters, inventors Orville and Wilbur Wright continued to improve their design. Soon they got a break.

On August 1, 1907, under orders from President Theodore Roosevelt, Army officials quietly created the Aeronautical Division of the United States Signal Corps. The mission of the new division was "to study the flying machine and the possibility of adapting it to military purposes."

A call went out to builders interested in constructing the world's first warplane. It had to seat two people with "a combined weight of 350 pounds", stow enough fuel for a 125-mile flight, be able to fly nonstop for a minimum of one hour, and reach a speed of at least 40 miles per hour in still air.

The Wright Brothers submitted a bid and signed a contract with the Signal Corps in February 1908 for $25,000. Suddenly, European countries became interested in the Wrights. Observing the first flights of the new war machine, a British official remarked that "Wilbur Wright is in possession of a power which controls the fate of nations."

Airplanes Go to War

The airplane's first military uses were in *reconnaissance*—observation and information gathering. In 1911, Italy carried out the first recorded use of an airplane for bombing. During a war with the Turks, an Italian pilot flew over a group of enemy soldiers and heaved a bomb at them.

Two pieces of warmaking machinery, the airplane and the machine gun, came together for the first time on June 7, 1912, when the gun was fired from an airplane at College Park, Maryland. Yet two years later at the start of World War I, Britain, France, and Germany had only modest air forces which were far from battle-ready. For ammunition, pilots used shotguns and bags of bricks, and then used machine guns. One World War I British pilot distinguished himself by being the first to bring down a reconnaissance balloon. The hydrogen explosion seriously damaged his own aircraft.

After several crashes and mishaps, Britain's Royal Air Corps (RAC) scored an historic victory. In September 1914, the RAC provided reconnaissance that thwarted the conquest of Paris by the Germans at the Battle of the Marne. A grateful Army commander on the ground reported: "Fired at constantly by both friend and foe, and not hesitating to fly in every kind of weather, they [the RAC] have remained undaunted throughout."

Combined with new radio technology, the warplane also proved its worth by enabling pilots to transmit enemy locations to artillery units for targeting. Reconnaissance aircraft flew over the battlefields at the front lines. Armies now had to find ways to keep the planes away in order to keep their locations and formations secret. For the first time in history, aerial dogfights became a part of war tactics.

The new airplane captured the imagination of people around the world. Only six years after the Wrights' historic flight, biplanes, a monoplane, and a dirigible entertain the crowd at an air show in France.

The Dogfight

It was a deadly duel. Unlike the clashes of large armies, the dogfight was one on one—rival pilots trying to shoot each other out of the sky. The dogfights of World War I captured public attention around the world and became legends of the twentieth century.

The biplane of the Wright Brothers' design, with its two parallel sets of wings, remained the Allies' airplane of choice throughout the war, despite the invention of the single-winged monoplane. Fighter pilots in clumsy but increasingly sophisticated aircraft became skilled at veering, climbing, and diving to out-maneuver one another. Pilots who officially downed five enemy planes earned the distinction of *flying ace*, a title that denoted recognition and respect.

The Red Baron

To 80 unlucky Allied dogfighters, catastrophe came in the color red—red like a firebird, swooping down on them with deadly aim. In his red Fokker three-winged triplane, Manfred von Richthofen was the most sought-after German pilot in the sky. The wealthy baron had fought on horseback and on foot before distinguishing himself in the Imperial Air Service. Leading a squadron of bright red planes known as "Richthofen's Flying Circus," he acquired the legendary nickname "the Red Baron."

The baron helped Germany's air corps dominate all others for much of World War I. He was there during "Bloody April", 1917, when the Germans shot down 368 British fighters. Twenty-one of them were credited to Richthofen. A horrifying 44 of Britain's finest flyers and aircraft went down in a single day, April 6.

But something else happened in April 1917, and it would end German control of the skies. The United States declared war on Germany.

Americans at War

The United States tried to remain neutral in World War I. Repeated German submarine attacks, however, on passenger and cargo ships in the Atlantic Ocean led to an American declaration of war on April 6, 1917.

United States soldiers and pilots proved to be good fighters and, along with abundant supplies of food and war goods, provided the edge needed to overcome the German threat. America's answer to the Red Baron was Eddie Rickenbacker, the nation's most renowned World War I flying ace. In his memoirs, entitled *Fighting the Flying Circus* (1919), Rickenbacker gave his view of the air corps' greatest contribution. He told the story of an Army unit that had been ambushed and sprayed with poison gas:

"One single preliminary airplane flight over this area before beginning the offensive would have disclosed to our troops the whole situation. In fact, I believe this function of 'seeing for the Army' is the most important one that belongs to the aviation arm in warfare. Bombing, patrolling, and bringing down enemy airplanes are but trivial compared to the vast importance of knowing the exact positions of the enemy's forces. . . ." Rickenbacker's opinion illustrates the priority of World War I airmen—reconnaissance.

Trivial or not, in just six months in the air, Rickenbacker scored 26 victories. His soaring career was halted only by the end of the war.

And the Red Baron? He was shot down and killed in combat on April 21, 1918. The baron's bravery had earned such wide admiration that the Royal Air Corps buried him with full military honors.

Victory at Last

Germany signed a truce with the Allies on November 11, 1918. Allied airplanes had played only a minor part in Germany's defeat. However, a few military leaders recognized the airplane's potential and envisioned a far greater role for air power in future wars.

Manfred von Richthofen, "the Red Baron"

British fighters (marked with bullseyes) swoop by German planes (identified by crosses) in this dizzying aerial view of a World War I dogfight.

Why did dogfights have a limited impact on the course of the war?

Should the United States build airplanes to use in war?

It is hard to imagine a time when the United States did not have an Air Force. The military uses of airplanes are evident today, but at the end of World War I, airplanes had not proven to everyone their value in battle. After World War I, leaders wrestled with the question of whether to develop new aviation technology for war when its value was unproven and new wars seemed unthinkable.

After the fighting ended, many Americans came to believe that involvement in World War I had been a mistake not to be repeated. The Senate rejected the Treaty of Versailles because senators did not wish to bind the United States to a League of Nations that could bring Americans into war against their will. President Warren G. Harding, who succeeded Woodrow Wilson in 1921, pursued a policy of isolationism, under which the United States would remain neutral in the affairs of other countries. Harding vowed that Americans would "seek no part in directing the destinies of the Old World. We do not mean to be entangled." With no intention of getting involved in events on the world stage, people questioned whether the United States should spend money to develop new technology for war, particularly when air power had played a minimal role in World War I.

> "We do not mean to be entangled."
>
> —*President Warren G. Harding, 1921*

With an isolationist foreign policy, America's only need for armed forces would be to defend against attack. Most experts believed that any threat to the security of the United States would come by sea. A well-developed navy would provide enough protection for the United States and spare the manpower and financial costs of a large army.

Air combat promised a new style of battle, with the potential to cause more devastation than traditional forms of land and sea warfare. Developing new weapons could have proven unpopular in a world rebuilding from the large-scale destruction of World War I. Americans and Europeans alike hoped that the devastation of the First World War would discourage any country from starting a war.

While the United States focused its attentions toward home in the 1920s, Britain, France, and Italy improved and expanded their air forces. Britain, France, Spain, and Italy used air power in their colonial empires not long after World War I ended.

World War I had been called "the war to end all wars," but the situation in Europe began to heat up again in the 1930s. Fascist leaders in Italy and Germany gained power on promises to avenge disappointments from the first war and win new territories in Europe and empires abroad. As they re-armed, they integrated air power into their war plans. In 1935, Italian dictator Benito Mussolini created an Italian air force, the Regia Aeronautica, as a symbol of Italian power and a future weapon of war. Minister of Aviation Italo Balbo staged demonstrations of Italian aviation involving large numbers of planes flying long distances in formation to impress foreign countries. German Chancellor Adolf Hitler officially re-established the German Air Force in violation of the Treaty of Versailles.

Britain flew the first Hawker Hart biplane in 1928. Faster and more advanced than WWI planes, Hart fighters and light bombers served British and foreign air forces well into the 1930s.

Air power would be used with devastating results in the Spanish Civil War, which broke out in 1936.

As leaders in the United States observed events in Europe in the 1930s, they considered whether the United States could afford to lag behind potential enemies in a new and crucial arena of battle. Hitler's attack on Poland in 1939 brought urgency to the question of investing in new aircraft. Hitler used his air forces in combination with land troops to take Poland with deadly speed. The United States could wait no longer to develop an air force. Worried by the specter of war, President Roosevelt authorized a massive buildup of the Army Air Corps in 1939.

Making a Decision

Use the following steps below to evaluate the decision to postpone investment in new aircraft. As you read each step, think of the important issues raised by the debate over building new aircraft for war.

◆ **Identify the problem and express it clearly.** First, determine whether a decision is needed; then clarify what needs to be decided. What is the issue you want to resolve or the goal you want to achieve? Describe the two opposing viewpoints in this debate in your own words.

◆ **Gather Information.** Find out facts about the issue. Be sure that your sources are reliable. List two facts and one opinion for each side in this debate.

◆ **Identify options.** Be sure to consider all the ways an issue might be handled. Stating the options clearly will help you decide. Describe the options faced by the United States government and the United States military in this debate.

◆ **Predicting consequences.** Identify the pros and cons of each choice. List one advantange and one disadvantage of each option.

◆ **Make a decision.** Evaluate your options; choose the one with the most acceptable consequences. Describe the choice made by the United States government with regard to aircraft for the military and explain why this was considered the best choice.

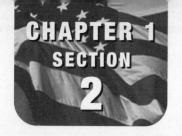

World War II

War Engulfs Europe

When the United States entered World War I, President Woodrow Wilson expressed his belief that the this conflict would be the "war to end all wars." But the Great War did not end wars. In fact, the events following that conflict helped launch an even more deadly worldwide war.

Peace in Europe brought only temporary comfort and security. Much of France and Belgium lay in ruins. Many nations were burdened by huge debts because they had borrowed heavily to pay for the war. Veterans returning to their homes in Europe could not find jobs. A modest economic recovery began to take hold in the 1920s, but it was shattered by the worldwide dive into the Great Depression of the 1930s.

Seeds of Discontent in Europe

Politically, World War I had done little to settle disputes. The Allies forced harsh penalties on Germany, requiring the country to pay huge sums of money for war damages. Although the Germans had not seen their country invaded or damaged by war, their leaders sued for peace when the tide of battle turned decisively against them.

Italy, a former Allied power, emerged from the war as a victor. But many Italians did not feel that their sacrifices had brought sufficient reward. Allied promises of new territory were not honored after the war ended. Italians suffered much like their former enemies did. Food riots and labor strikes as early as 1919 brought fear and chaos to the country.

Fascists Take Power

Fascism is a system of government characterized by dictatorship, belligerent nationalism, and militarism. The Nazis are a well-known example of a fascist group. After World War I, many countries urgently needed effective leaders to rebuild. Poor national economies made countries ripe for unrest, conditions seized upon by radical politicians who fed on peoples' fears and resentments. In Italy and Germany, fascist leaders came to power by recalling past power and glory and by blaming scapegoats for present problems.

In the 1920s, Benito Mussolini rejected democracy and used violence to eliminate old leaders and seize power in Italy. In Germany, Adolf Hitler declared that Germany "will rise again!" In spellbinding speeches, he declared that Germans belonged to a master race of "Aryan" Europeans destined to rule the world, and that Germany lost World War I because, in his view, it was "stabbed in the back" by Jews. In an era of economic despair and street battles between Nazis and Communists, Hitler became Chancellor in 1933.

Mussolini and Hitler each ruled as *dictators*, leaders with absolute power. They each began an enormous military buildup of armies and weapons and agreed to cooperate in a violent campaign to terrorize and control Europe. More importantly, they included new air forces in their plans.

Hermann Goering, commander of Germany's new air force and a committed Nazi, leads a Nazi march.

A New Power in Asia

Half a world away, military leaders in Japan had their own plans for conquest and empire. In 1931, Japan's forces easily captured China's vast northern province of Manchuria. Six years later, the Japanese brutally overran much of eastern China. Protests from Western democracies had no effect.

Perceiving the weaknesses of Western democracies, Germany, Italy, and Japan created an alliance known as the Axis Powers. By the late 1930s, the clock was ticking toward war.

Spain: A Training Ground

To Hitler's prey, time was no friend. The military buildup in Europe intensified in the 1930s, thanks to new technology, which the Nazis used to their advantage. When German troops invaded France in World War I, French forces had time to retreat to Paris and reorganize while the Germans advanced slowly on the ground over several weeks. The next war would move to a faster clock. New sophisticated airplanes as well as tanks would allow Germany to lash out like a fanged cobra, giving its victims little chance to resist. From the start, Hitler saw the potential of air power. By 1939, he had at his service some 1,000 fighter planes and 1,050 bombers.

The Luftwaffe

Long before war broke out again, Germany's best scientific minds were working furiously to design a new generation of machines for modern battle. Faster tanks with protective armor were built to mow through the European countryside. A new fleet of Nazi submarines would make the seas more dangerous for Allied ships in the event of war.

Since World War I, aircraft technology had been rapidly improving, and the Germans took it to new heights, literally. Old wood-and-fabric biplanes looked like toys compared with the sleek, metal monoplanes with enclosed cockpits. Germany's air force, the Luftwaffe, had fighter planes that were as fast and well-armed as anything Britain had. It would be Germany's main weapon in the coming Battle of Britain.

Guernica

Hitler experimented with air power in the Spanish Civil War (1936–1939), ensuring the triumph of another dictator, Francisco Franco. One of the worst horrors was a German air raid on the Spanish market town of Guernica on

> ## "A preview of the end of the world"
>
> —*Description of the Guernica raid by an observer in the hills*

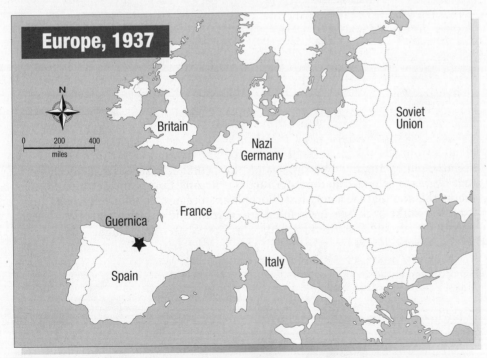

Europe, 1937

N

0   200   400
miles

Britain

Nazi Germany

Soviet Union

Guernica

France

Spain

Italy

Civil war in Spain, a poor country on the fringe of Europe, drew in important players from all over the continent. Nazi Germany and Italy supported the Nationalist forces of Spanish General Franco with military intervention, while the Soviet Union sent aid to the Republican government. Britain and France watched uneasily but refused to become too deeply involved.

Why did the bombing of Guernica alarm people outside of Spain?

April 25, 1937. The attack was initiated by Colonel Wolfram von Richthofen, a cousin of "the Red Baron." Richthofen argued, "Morale is more important in winning battles than weapons. Continuously repeated, concentrated air attacks have the most effect on the morale of the enemy."

The Nazis tried out their air power on the civilian town with more than 40 aircraft. Junkers Ju-52s bombed the town every 15 minutes as biplanes swooped in low to gun down any survivors.

The Nazi "experiment" killed some 1,600 innocent civilians. Guernica alerted Europe and the United States to the potential for massive bombing raids directed against cities.

Blitzkrieg: The Lightning War

After massive rearmament from 1935 to 1939, Germany was ready to flex its military might. Hitler maneuvered to seize control of Austria in 1938 and of democratic Czechoslovakia by 1939. Britain and France were reluctant to go to war and repeatedly appeased Germany although their combined militaries were much stronger than Hitler's forces.

Then, on September 1, 1939, Nazi forces stormed into Poland, revealing the incredible power of Hitler's *blitzkrieg*, or "lightning war." In a pattern that would be repeated successfully throughout Europe, German planes bombed airfields, factories, and undefended cities and towns in the first days of battle. Dive bombers bombed Polish soldiers and civilians to stir up fear and confusion. The air strikes cleared the way for fast-moving tanks and motorized troop carriers to roar across the country. The overpowered Polish Army retreated to defend the capital, Warsaw. When the Soviet Union invaded from the east on September 17, Poland's fate was sealed.

War!

British Prime Minister Neville Chamberlain's appeasement of Hitler had failed. On September 3, Britain and France declared war on Germany. However, Poland fell too quickly for the Allies to intervene. Neither side moved during the winter of 1939–1940.

Hitler overran Denmark and Norway in April 1940. On May 10, he launched a surprise attack against the Netherlands, Belgium, Luxembourg, and France with the full weight of 2.2 million soldiers supported by 3,500 combat aircraft. German tanks bypassed France's main lines of defense and broke through French lines near the city of Sedan. The French were unable to regroup and stop the Germans. British forces fell back to the English Channel port of Dunkirk. With a heroic effort, the Royal Navy and thousands of British volunteers in small boats evacuated more than 338,000 British and French soldiers from the beaches of Dunkirk to England. The Luftwaffe was unable to stop the evacuation, despite bombing the beaches. The Royal Air Force (RAF) shot down enemy fighter planes and bombers and thwarted their bomb runs. Many of the bombs fell into soft mud or sand and were rendered nearly harmless. Much of the evacuation was carried out at night.

German troops marched into Paris on June 14, only five weeks after the offensive began. Hitler, triumphant, forced the French to sign a document of surrender in the same railroad car in which Germany signed an armistice in 1918. Britain alone faced Germany and its powerful air force, the Luftwaffe.

Messerschmitt 109 fighter plane

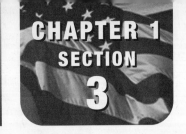

Britain Under Siege

The Battle of Britain

After France, the big territorial prize Germany hoped to claim was Britain. The Nazi effort to conquer Britain produced the first prolonged air engagement in history, and Hitler's first major defeat.

Alone to face the Nazi war machine, Great Britain was saved from immediate conquest by a narrow stretch of water and by the courage of the British, led by Prime Minister Winston Churchill, to fight no matter the odds. The English Channel, only 21 miles in width at its narrowest point, separates England from the coast of France. (See map, page 21.) Since ancient times, the Channel had often turned back invaders. But in 1940, as German troops stood on the French shore and looked across the water, Hitler prepared to overcome this geographic barrier in a new way: by airplane.

In the spring of 1940, the first German air squadrons flew over the English Channel, beginning one of the greatest war dramas in history: the Battle of Britain. In London, Britain's new and fiery prime minister, Winston Churchill, issued a battle cry:

> "We shall defend our island, whatever the cost may be. We shall fight on the beaches, we shall fight on the landing grounds, we shall fight in the fields and in the streets, we shall fight in the hills; we shall never surrender."
>
> —*Winston Churchill, radio address, June 4, 1940*

Invasion by Air

The Nazis' invasion plan called for a massive bombing campaign to pave the way for a cross-channel landing of the German army. The first targets for destruction were ports, radar stations, and Royal Air Force (RAF) airfields. Destroying the radar stations and airfields would prevent the RAF from defending the island against an invasion. The Luftwaffe onslaught was fierce, but the Germans had underestimated a critical factor: the courage and determination of Britain's pilots.

The RAF threw planes and pilots into battle, mounting a defense that Hitler could not overcome. British flyers had two technological allies. One

---

Science Link   How Radar Helped Save England

When German bomber aircraft bore down on English cities, they encountered an invisible weapon. From tall towers up and down the coast of England and Scotland, radar stations sent out signals that detected the presence of incoming bombers as far as 150 miles away.

Radar (a term coined from "radio detecting and ranging") is an instrument that transmits electromagnetic beams in various directions. A beam bounces off objects in its path and sends an "echo" back to a receiver. The radar determines the distance of an object by measuring the time it took for the beam to go out and to return. By sending out a series of sig-

nals, radar can often predict the path of the object. The system can calculate the size and shape of objects.

Practical development of radar dates back to experiments on electromagnetic radiation by German physicist Heinrich Hertz in the late 1880s. By 1939, all the major Allied and Axis nations had some form of military radar, but the Luftwaffe failed to fully recognize the strategic value of radar, until radar warned the RAF of attacks and gave its fighter squadrons enough time to get high enough into the air to confront the Luftwaffe on its daytime raids.

Question: *What advantage(s) did radar give Britain during German attacks?*

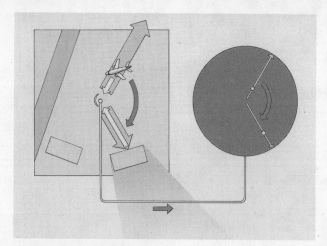

Radar beams (wide arrows) travel from a central point until they hit an object and return to the receiver. The time it takes for the signal to return indicates the airplane's distance. The airplane appears as a dot of light on the display (right).

was the "eyes and ears" of Britain: radar, the world's most advanced warning system. The other weapon was the new Spitfire, a speedy and maneuverable fighter that would serve Britain throughout World War II and become the star of the RAF.

The German attack plan included bombers to destroy targets on the ground and fighters to challenge RAF fighters and protect the bombers from attack. In action this plan suffered serious flaws. German bombers lacked the bomb-load capacity to strike a permanent knock-out punch to Britain. German fighter escorts lacked the fuel capacity to fly far enough from their bases in Europe to defend the bombers. In addition, radar deprived the attackers of the element of surprise, and for these reasons German bombers proved to be vulnerable to RAF fighters in daylight.

Britain Turns the Tide

The British Spitfires owed some of their effectiveness to American James H. Doolittle, who was later to become commander of the U.S. Eighth Air Force. In the 1930s, he had worked for Shell Oil Company and had encouraged the creation of higher-grade 100 octane fuel. The better fuel resulted in a 3 percent increase in power for the RAF Spitfires, giving them an advantage in facing the German Me-109. In addition, the Spitfire's low wing loading enabled it to out-maneuver the Me-109.

But it was more than fuel that fired the British air fleet: It was the persistence, bravery, and skill of the fliers, some of them American volunteers, who came back again and again to challenge the supposedly invincible Luftwaffe. The RAF suffered dramatic losses, but the Luftwaffe fared worse.

Winston Churchill acknowledged the bravery of these airmen in his immortal statement: "Never in the field of human conflict was so much owed by so many to so few."

The RAF resistance was so fierce that the Luftwaffe switched from daytime bombing to night raids, when RAF fighters could not be as effective. The night raids did not defeat Britain. By September, Hitler was forced to put his invasion plans on hold. Although the Luftwaffe was on the verge of destroying the RAF airfields, in a strategic blunder the Luftwaffe abandoned attacks on radar stations and airfields, and took the battle to London itself. This last, desperate campaign to bring Britain to its knees became known as the Blitz.

The Blitz

The Luftwaffe's top commanders could see the famous white cliffs of Dover, England, as they dined in fine style across the channel at Calais, France, on September 7, 1940. They felt the ground rumble underneath them as 348 heavy bombers and 600 escort fighters droned above them, blackening the sky on a course for London that evening. The men in the dining room were pleased.

An RAF pilot in the air above London saw menace approaching:

"[A]ll we could see was row upon row of German raiders heading for London. I have never seen so many aircraft in the air all at the same time. . . . The escorting fighters saw us at once and came down like a ton of bricks, when the squadron split up and the sky became a seething cauldron of aeroplanes. . . ."

—*RAF Squadron Leader A. V. R. Johnstone, 602nd Squadron*

London's St. Paul's Cathedral survived the Battle of Britain, while surrounding buildings were reduced to rubble.

Throughout the night, waves of enemy aircraft showered high explosives and firebombs on the sprawling capital. The bombing continued for 57 nights. It turned large areas of the city into smoking ruins and killed roughly 15,000 people. Infuriated by Hitler's deadly strike at England's civilian population, Churchill ordered bombers to Berlin. That attack further intensified Nazi aggression against British cities.

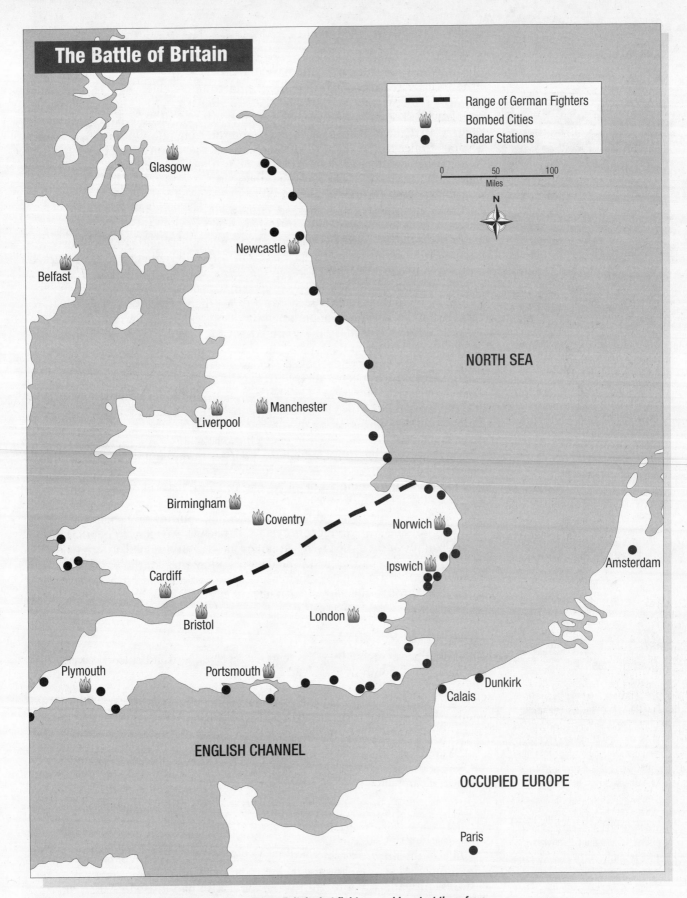

The Battle of Britain

- - - Range of German Fighters

Bombed Cities

● Radar Stations

0   50   100
Miles

N

Glasgow

Belfast

Newcastle

NORTH SEA

Liverpool   Manchester

Birmingham

Coventry

Norwich

Ipswich

Cardiff

Bristol

London

Amsterdam

Plymouth

Portsmouth

Dunkirk

Calais

ENGLISH CHANNEL

OCCUPIED EUROPE

Paris

German bombers attacked airfields and cities all over Britain, but fighters could protect them from British counterattacks in only the southeast. Radar stations along the coast sensed the arrival of German planes over the water and gave the RAF enough warning time to take to the air in defense.

What were two possible reasons why London was a tempting target for the Luftwaffe?

Great Britain Unites

The people of London will forever be remembered for their unbreakable spirit during months of horror. In a remarkable program already well underway, Britain evacuated more than 2 million children under the age of 15, pregnant mothers, the deaf and the blind, mothers of children under 5 years old, and people with severe disabilities to the countryside. People dug backyard bomb shelters. Parliament continued to meet, and the King and Queen refused suggestions to flee to the countryside—or Canada—for protection. Londoners went to shelters during the frequent air raids, then emerged when the all-clear signal sounded to carry on with their lives.

Workers rescued more than 256,000 pets from the bombings. The nation's art treasures, including paintings, sculptures, and priceless china, went into safekeeping in shelters or mines, or were sent out of the country.

At night the city enforced a blackout, banning most lighting to prevent bombers from seeing their targets. Buses ran without headlights; citizens blacked out their windows. American war reporter Ernie Pyle described his arrival in London at night when the city was draped in darkness. The blackout was "like something mysterious, darkly seen in a dream—shapes here, shadows there, tiny lights swimming toward you, dark bulks moving noiselessly away."

Peter Armitage lived on the south coast of England, where the bombs first fell. At the innocent age of 10, he had already learned how to identify aircraft. He and his friends looked forward to the excitement.

"Each night we spent several hours in the air raid shelter in the field next to our housing development. The shelter was nothing but a big trench cut into the ground and covered with corrugated iron sheets and earth; dark, damp, and filled with steel bunks—bring your own mattress and blankets. As if anyone could actually sleep with all the ack-ack noise going on! . . . We kids had no sense of the gravity and danger in our situation; it was all excitement to us."

In late 1940, the family got an enormous scare. Several days of rain had provided temporary relief from the nightly bombing attacks. "When the weather cleared, the night raiders came back, but our air raid shelter in the field was flooded with about four feet of water. We stayed at home that night spending a lot of the time crouched under the stairs. No one had been able to go to the shelter in the field. The next morning after all the air activity, we found that our safe haven shelter had sustained a direct hit, with a bomb going right through the entrance." They never returned to the shelter in the field.

The Spirit of Defiance

One Londoner expressed the tremendous resolve that the British showed throughout the bombings:

"Night after night, night after night, the bombardment of London continues. . . . I am nerveless, and yet I am conscious that when I hear a motor in the empty streets I tauten myself lest it be a bomb screaming towards me . . . . There is a lull now. The guns die down towards the horizon like a thunderstorm passing to the south. But they will come back again in fifteen minutes. We are conscious all the time that this is a moment in history. I have a sense of strain and unhappiness; but none of fear. One feels so proud."

—*diary of Harold Nicolson, September 19, 1940*

Or, as another proud Londoner put it, Germany "will run out of bombs before we run out of courage."

Indeed, the Blitz did not end so much as wither away. On September 17, 1940, Hitler secretly postponed the invasion of Britain. The Battle of Britain cost the Luftwaffe 1,700 aircraft while the British had lost only 900 fighters. The Luftwaffe continued sporadic bombing through May, 1941, but the effort was not worth the results. It was a costly defeat; nevertheless, Hitler's appetite and ability to wage war remained undiminished.

Prime Minister Winston Churchill

Character Values

Cheerfulness

During the Blitz, the strength of the human spirit prevailed over the German assault. At night, under fire, Londoners kept up their spirits with games, songs, and conversation, drawing family and friends closer together. Their cheerfulness proved to be a powerful weapon against the Blitz. A positive outlook was a character trait that enabled the British to turn the tide of war and defeat Germany.

The American Response

From the start of the Nazi nightmare, Americans followed the grim news, but the majority had no taste for involvement in Europe's troubles. Plenty of people could still remember the suffering in Europe during World War I. They were in no hurry to send their young men into combat for Europe again. The prevailing view was to let Britain and France take care of Germany.

President Franklin Delano Roosevelt was sensitive to the public's desire to stay out of the world's troubles. The day that Britain and France declared war, he tried to reassure Americans in a radio address:

> "This nation will remain a neutral nation, but I cannot ask that every American remain neutral in thought as well. . . . I have said not once but many times that I have seen war and that I hate war. . . . I hope that the United States will keep out of this war."
>
> —*President Roosevelt, fireside chat, September 3, 1939*

This statement revealed Roosevelt's own deep sympathies and worries about the war and about America's responsibility to come to the aid of the Allies. With the Battle of Britain raging, Roosevelt feared catastrophic global effects if Hitler were to capture the mammoth British Royal Navy. Hitler's hunger for empire became even more apparent in June 1941 when his forces attacked the Soviet Union in violation of Germany's solemn non-aggression pact with the Soviet Union.

Despite his reassurances of American neutrality, the President began gradually preparing Americans to accept the necessity of war. In September 1940, Roosevelt ordered the first peacetime draft (required service in the military) ever. Some young men waited for the order to arrive in the mail. Others leaped at the opportunity to serve and volunteered immediately. The nation could not imagine that it would soon be drawn into the conflict.

Members of the "Mother's Crusade" knelt and prayed outside the Capitol to stop Congress from passing Bill 1776, known as the Lend-Lease Act.

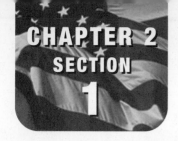

CHAPTER 2
SECTION 1

A Call to Arms

Pearl Harbor

United States Naval Base, Pearl Harbor, Hawaii: a dream assignment for young sailors, airmen, nurses, and other lucky military personnel. This is a Pacific paradise on the south coast of the island of Oahu. Palm trees, waters of crystal, surf and sand, the sweet perfumes of exotic flowers—all while serving Uncle Sam.

Of course, everyone hears about the evil being inflicted on Europe by a German madman. But on the radio, the President says he's keeping America out of that war. Besides, that crisis is so far, far away, and the balmy blanket of a Hawaiian night feels warm and safe. As day breaks on Sunday, December 7, 1941, a cloud cover melts away into infinite blue skies. It is, as one sailor remembers it, "one more beautiful day in paradise." Indeed, this is heaven on earth.

Forget heaven.

With death on its wings, the best of the Japanese naval air force streaks toward an unsuspecting Pearl Harbor. Even the warning sirens stay in quiet slumber until, at 7:55 A.M, a low droning noise rises into a deafening roar. Men and women in sleepy numbness fling themselves out of their beds and run toward their battle positions, as their training has taught them. In horror, they see a sky dense with aircraft that are not their own. Bullets from strafing aircraft strike the ground and giant explosions suck the very air from their lungs. Shaking off disbelief, they grasp the slow-dawning truth that this is no training drill. Americans, on American soil, are under attack.

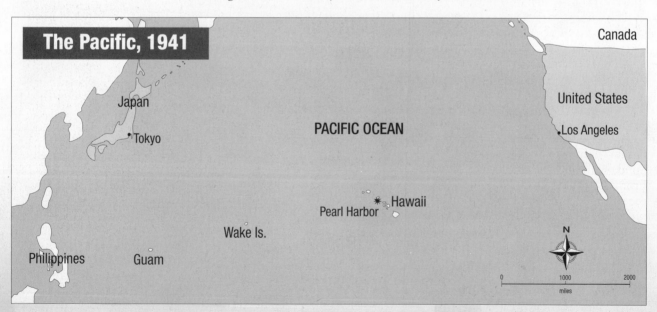

On December 7, Japan launched surprise attacks on several American bases in the Pacific Ocean.
Why do you think Japan felt confident in attacking these American bases?

Honoring the American Past

Trouble in Paradise

American relations with Japan had soured ever since the Japanese invasion of China in the 1930s. When war broke out in Europe in 1939, the resource-poor Japanese saw a chance to grab European territories in Southeast Asia. The region's large reserves of oil, rubber, and tin would help in the conquest of China. As Japanese aggression expanded into Southeast Asia, the United States moved to cut off shipments to Japan of critical supplies, such as scrap metal and oil. Japan was enraged at U.S. interference with their plans of conquest.

To President Roosevelt and his top staff, the course was plain by late November 1941. There would be war—perhaps within days; at least by Christmas, they reckoned. Quietly, a war warning went out to the army and navy commanders at Pearl Harbor, where a majority of ships in America's naval fleet and several hundred aircraft were stationed. These were only general warnings that did not raise alert levels. In the meantime, Japanese diplomats continued to negotiate with their American counterparts in Washington to resolve their tensions. The government knew that Japan was only stalling for time, but they could not be certain of attack plans.

Some American strategists correctly predicted the outbreak of war on Sunday, December 7. But most expected the first clash to occur at American bases much farther west, perhaps in the South Pacific. Commanders at Pearl Harbor busily prepared their fleet to sail westward and engage the Japanese navy in battle. In their efforts, they made few defensive preparations.

Japan Attacks

The meticulously prepared Japanese mission planned first to destroy U.S. aircraft on the ground to minimize an air defense. Then, the bombers would strike at the ships lined up at "Battleship Row" with torpedoes that were modified to run in Pearl Harbor's shallow waters.

A teletype machine communicated news of the attack to Washington, D.C.

December 6–7 happened to be the first weekend in five months that all battleships were in port at once. Throughout the sprawling base, men and women planned Sunday activities—going to church, to the beach, to a tennis tournament. Others took the chance to sleep in. Many sailors had gone ashore for the weekend. Aircraft sat, many unfueled, on the parking aprons; most of the anti-aircraft gunners were getting the day off, too.

Radio operator Emery Morrison had no leisure plans. He was on duty that Sunday, aboard the cruiser U.S.S. *Raleigh*. From the railing at midship, he gazed in the distance and saw airplanes diving and puffs of smoke rising from the airfields.

"My thought was, what a strange time of day for a drill that realistic," Morrison recalls. Moments later a plane dived straight at the *Raleigh*. "I could clearly see the pilot, the plane with its large red ball on the side [the symbol of Japan], and the rear gunner . . . looking at me as I stared at him. Before it could register that the plane was Japanese, there was a terrific explosion almost under me."

He was thrown several feet into a metal door. "I sat on the deck . . . dazed, trying to understand what had just happened."

Pearl Harbor Under Fire

For many of the pilots on the bases and sailors on duty along "Battleship Row," there was no time to think, or even to move. Despite heroic efforts by pilots to get to their planes amid the gunfire, the attack happened so quickly that few aircraft managed to get off the ground. A few pilots daringly pursued the enemy and shot down a number of Japanese planes before they could inflict more damage.

The first wave of Japanese attackers consisted of 183 aircraft, including 40 torpedo planes, 49 horizontal bombers, 51 dive bombers, and 43 fighters. After a pause of about 20 minutes, the second wave bore down on the damaged ships: 170 aircraft, consisting of 54 horizontal bombers, 80 dive bombers, and 36 fighters. Japanese naval support included 4 aircraft carriers, 4 cruisers, 35 submarines, 2 battleships, and 11 destroyers.

An explosion rocked the U.S.S. *Arizona*, and the ship heaved upward and then plunged to the bottom of the harbor, instantly taking more than 1,100 men to their watery grave.

U.S. Personnel Casualties

Service	Killed	Wounded
Navy	2,008	710
Army	218	364
Marines	109	69
Civilians	68	35
Total	2,403	1,178

U.S. Aircraft Damage

Service	Lost	Damaged
Army	77	128
Navy	92	31

The Pearl Harbor attack took the lives of over 2,000 Americans.

Sailors React

As their ships rocked and tilted toward the water, sailors, including the wounded, scrambled to their battle stations, taking aim at the enemy attackers, two of five midget enemy submarines entered the harbor, but were sunk and did not release any torpedoes at U.S. targets.

Tornadoes of fire swept through the ships, forcing reluctant crews to abandon many of them. Men, some badly burned, jumped into the water and tried to swim to safety, but the water had turned to fire, as oil and fuel spilled into the harbor, floated to the surface, and burned. When the bombing ceased and the last attackers disappeared from view, Japan had destroyed or damaged 18 American ships, disabled hundreds of aircraft, killed more than 2,400 and wounded 1,178 people.

A nation now headed for war would have to begin with a drastically reduced navy. Only the navy's aircraft carriers, safely away from Pearl Harbor on December 7, remained intact. The *Saratoga* was docked in San Diego after an overhaul. The *Lexington* was 425 miles southeast of Midway Island in the Central Pacific, and the *Enterprise* was returning from a trip to Wake Island when the attack began. Significantly, the loss of battleships would force the navy to rely more on its aircraft carriers, and therefore on air power itself.

Literature Link

Compare these two passages, written in reaction to the attack on Pearl Harbor on December 7 (December 8 in Japan, which is on the other side of the international date line).

Yesterday, December 7, 1941—a date which will live in infamy—the United States of America was suddenly and deliberately attacked by naval and air forces of the Empire of Japan. …Hostilities exist. There is no blinking at the fact that our people, our territory and our interests are in grave danger…. With confidence in our armed forces—with the unbounded determination of our people—we will gain the inevitable triumph—so help us God.

—*President Franklin Delano Roosevelt, speech to the nation, December 8, 1941*

"Remember December eighth!
On this day the history of the world was changed.
The Anglo-Saxon powers
On this day were repulsed on Asian land and sea.
It was their Japan which repulsed them,
A tiny country in the Eastern Sea,
Nippon, the Land of the Gods
Ruled over by a living god."

—*Japanese poet Kotaro Takamura*

Questions: Why do FDR and Takamura urge their fellow citizens not to forget Pearl Harbor? How does each writer express confidence?

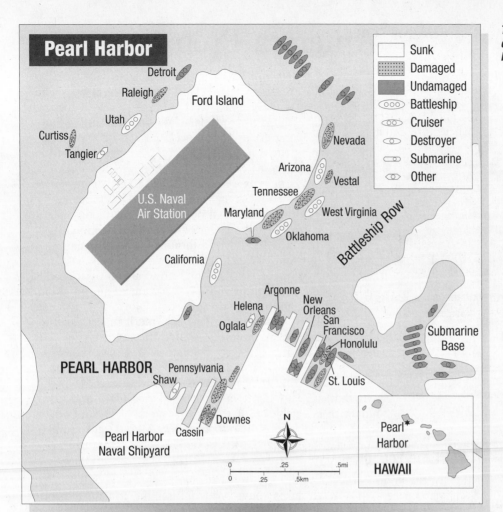

Pearl Harbor

Legend:
- Sunk
- Damaged
- Undamaged
- Battleship
- Cruiser
- Destroyer
- Submarine
- Other

The attack on Pearl Harbor decimated the American battleship fleet in the Pacific.

Map labels: Detroit, Raleigh, Utah, Curtiss, Tangier, Ford Island, U.S. Naval Air Station, Nevada, Arizona, Vestal, Tennessee, Maryland, West Virginia, Oklahoma, Battleship Row, California, Argonne, Helena, New Orleans, San Francisco, Honolulu, Oglala, St. Louis, Submarine Base, PEARL HARBOR, Pennsylvania, Shaw, Downes, Cassin, Pearl Harbor Naval Shipyard, Pearl Harbor, HAWAII

Scale: 0 .25 .5mi / 0 .25 .5km

Summary of U.S. Ship Damage

Ship	Summary	Rejoined Fleet	Ship	Summary	Rejoined Fleet
BATTLESHIPS			**DESTROYERS**		
Arizona	Sunk, total loss	No	Cassin	Heavily damaged, rebuilt	February 1944
California	Sunk, raised, repaired, modernized	May 1944	Curtiss	Damaged, repaired	January 1942
Maryland	Damaged, repaired, modernized	February 1942	Downes	Heavily damaged, rebuilt	November 1943
Nevada	Heavily damaged, grounded, refloated, repaired, modernized	December 1942	Helm	Damaged, continued on patrol, repaired	January 1942
Oklahoma	Capsized, total loss	No	**MINECRAFT**		
Pennsylvania	Slightly damaged, repaired, modernized	August 1942	Oglala	Sunk, raised, repaired	February 1944
Tennessee	Damaged, repaired	March 1942	**AUXILIARIES**		
Utah	Capsized, on bottom of Pearl Harbor	No	Sotoyomo	Sunk, raised, repaired	August 1942
West Virginia	Sunk, raised, repaired, modernized	July 1944	Vestal	Heavily damaged, beached, refloated, repaired	February 1942
CRUISERS			YFD-2	Sunk, raised, refloated, repaired	May 1942
Helena	Heavily damaged, repaired	June 1942			
Honolulu	Damaged, repaired, overhauled	January 1942			
Raleigh	Heavily damaged, repaired, overhauled	July 1942			

The government used this image of a flyer to sell war bonds.

America Prepares

On December 8 in Washington, D.C., President Roosevelt made a broadcast to the American people in which he declared that December 7, 1941 was "a date which will live in infamy." Japan had declared war on the United States and Britain. Congress promptly declared war on Japan. As allies of Japan, the other Axis Powers, Germany and Italy, joined the war against America.

Americans once divided over the issue of war now united as a nation, rallied by their President. On December 9, Roosevelt laid out a national policy for wartime. Production of weapons for the military had already been stepped up for more than a year, and he announced that "we have mustered our manpower to build up a new Army. . . ." Production of naval vessels would now be greatly increased. Aid shipments to Britain and naval patrols of shipping lanes in the submarine-infested waters of the North Atlantic were to be increased. Roosevelt called on Americans to assist in war readiness by making local preparations for civilian defense. The army and navy began building new bases nationwide.

Japanese Admiral Yamamoto said after Pearl Harbor, "I fear that we have but awakened a sleeping giant and filled him with a terrible resolve." Japan was soon to find out what America's mighty industrial power could accomplish.

A Wartime Economy

Much of the nation's economy immediately came under federal control. Upon Roosevelt's orders, industrial plants converted from making consumer products such as cars and refrigerators to making wartime goods. To raise money for war expenses, the government sold bonds and encouraged citizens to buy them. The government set the prices of many products, decided how much would be produced, and negotiated wages with labor unions.

 Math Link **How Bonds Work**

Waging war is an expensive proposition. To pay for war, a government can raise money through new taxes, cut spending on other programs, and borrow from banks and the public. The costs of World War II rose so high, so quickly, that they presented a special challenge.

Income taxes were raised, but there was a limit to how high rates could go. The new war budget was several times the size of a typical pre-war budget so there was little money to shift from existing programs. To raise the bulk of the money, the government borrowed from the people. In effect, it spread out the cost of the war over the decades to come by promising to pay back loans in the future.

President Roosevelt launched the war bond program in 1941. War bonds came in denominations from $25 to $10,000. People had money to spend on bonds. Because so few consumer goods were available, and many necessities rationed, people's bank accounts swelled. In mid-1943, Americans had some $70 billion in cash, checking accounts, and savings accounts, up from $50 billion in 1941.

An American would buy a $25 bond in 1942 at a discounted rate—perhaps $20. In exchange, the government promised to pay $25 when the bond had "matured" in ten or thirty years. The government now had $20 to spend on war costs. The bondholder had a safe investment for money he or she could not spend anyway. Both the government and the bondholder trusted that the war would be over by 1952 or 1972, when the government would pay back the loan with a profit for the bondholder.

Businesses purchased the main share of the $135 billion in bonds the government sold during World War II. About $36 billion of that, no small amount, was bought by individual Americans—not only helping to finance the war, but involving the public in the war effort as well.

Question: How were war bonds good for America and good for the war effort?

Before Pearl Harbor, Roosevelt had declared: "Defense today means more than merely fighting. It means morale, civilian as well as military; it means using every available resource; it means enlarging every useful plant. . . . Articles of defense must have undisputed right of way in every industrial plant in the country."

In the year to come, Americans—in banking, in business, in engineering, in construction—would build a remarkable 48,000 warplanes. Now, the task was to find the dedicated, steel-nerved men to fly them.

Aircraft had come a long way from their origins by the time the U.S. went to war in 1941. Brainstorm five words or phrases that describe the aircraft of 1941 in relation to the aircraft of 1914.

Biplanes to Bombers: A Technological Revolution

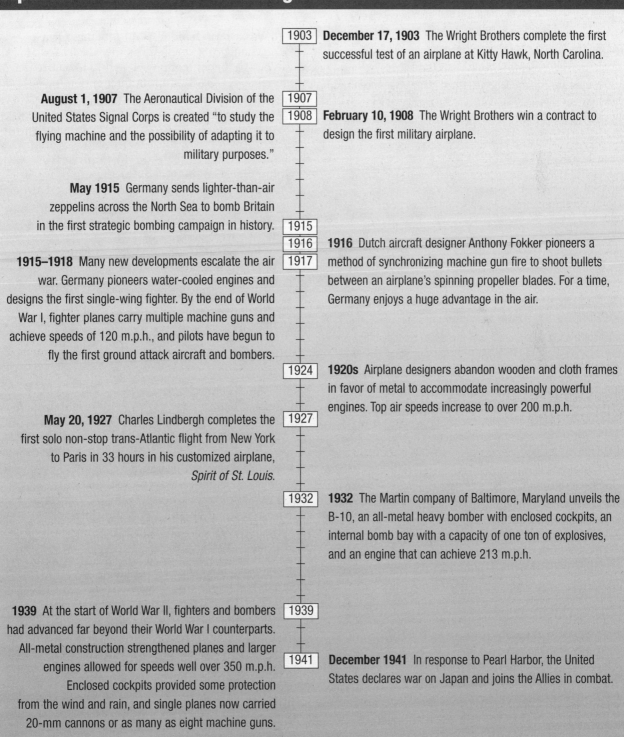

1903 — **December 17, 1903** The Wright Brothers complete the first successful test of an airplane at Kitty Hawk, North Carolina.

August 1, 1907 The Aeronautical Division of the United States Signal Corps is created "to study the flying machine and the possibility of adapting it to military purposes." — **1907**

1908 — **February 10, 1908** The Wright Brothers win a contract to design the first military airplane.

May 1915 Germany sends lighter-than-air zeppelins across the North Sea to bomb Britain in the first strategic bombing campaign in history. — **1915**

1916 — **1916** Dutch aircraft designer Anthony Fokker pioneers a method of synchronizing machine gun fire to shoot bullets between an airplane's spinning propeller blades. For a time, Germany enjoys a huge advantage in the air.

1915–1918 Many new developments escalate the air war. Germany pioneers water-cooled engines and designs the first single-wing fighter. By the end of World War I, fighter planes carry multiple machine guns and achieve speeds of 120 m.p.h., and pilots have begun to fly the first ground attack aircraft and bombers. — **1917**

1924 — **1920s** Airplane designers abandon wooden and cloth frames in favor of metal to accommodate increasingly powerful engines. Top air speeds increase to over 200 m.p.h.

May 20, 1927 Charles Lindbergh completes the first solo non-stop trans-Atlantic flight from New York to Paris in 33 hours in his customized airplane, *Spirit of St. Louis*. — **1927**

1932 — **1932** The Martin company of Baltimore, Maryland unveils the B-10, an all-metal heavy bomber with enclosed cockpits, an internal bomb bay with a capacity of one ton of explosives, and an engine that can achieve 213 m.p.h.

1939 At the start of World War II, fighters and bombers had advanced far beyond their World War I counterparts. All-metal construction strengthened planes and larger engines allowed for speeds well over 350 m.p.h. Enclosed cockpits provided some protection from the wind and rain, and single planes now carried 20-mm cannons or as many as eight machine guns. — **1939**

1941 — **December 1941** In response to Pearl Harbor, the United States declares war on Japan and joins the Allies in combat.

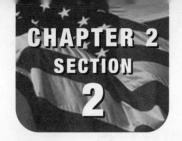

**CHAPTER 2
SECTION
2**

The Eighth Air Force

The Eighth Air Force was only one of 16 air forces in the Army Air Forces. Some of these forces fought with the Mighty Eighth against Nazi Germany. The Ninth Air Force first fought against the Nazis in North Africa and then moved to England in 1943 to fight over Europe and prepare for the invasion of France. The Twelfth and Fifteenth Air Forces flew missions against the Axis from bases in the Mediterranean.

The air war against Japan engaged many other forces. The Fifth and Thirteenth Air Forces in the southwest Pacific attacked Japan in New Guinea and the Philippines. The Tenth and the Fourteenth defended India and China. The Seventh Air Force defended Hawaii until 1943, when it went on the offensive in the Pacific. Similarly, the Eleventh Air Force changed from defending Alaska to fighting the Japanese in the Aleutian Islands. The Twentieth Air Force was the Pacific counterpart of the Mighty Eighth: a bomber force targeting the enemy on occupied territory and eventually at home. B-29 bombers of the Twentieth dropped the atomic bombs on Hiroshima and Nagasaki that brought an end to the war.

While forces fought in combat, five additional forces performed vital duties away from the front. The First, Second, and Fourth Air Forces trained new pilots and defended the mainland United States. In addition to training pilots, the Third defended the United States against submarines. The Sixth Air Force, stationed in Panama, targeted submarines and protected the vital Panama Canal.

The first home of the Eighth Air Force was the National Guard Armory in Savannah, Georgia.

The Men Who Dared to Fly

He was a farm hand in rural Indiana. Or a mechanic in a small Texas town. Perhaps a young student from New York. He had to get his parents' permission to join the military, or he might have changed the date on his birth certificate to appear to be old enough to enlist. He hadn't learned to drive a car. Yet in a few months the hometown boy, at the controls of a 32-ton heavy bomber, would wage the fight of his life in the skies over Europe.

John Veenschoten underwent the rapid transformation from innocent kid to battle-hardened airman. When he heard about Pearl Harbor, "I was still a senior in high school. . . . I was fascinated by the fact that we were going to war."

Veenschoten arrived in England in April 1944 and eagerly volunteered for his first mission. "[T]he anti-aircraft guns were firing and I thought, 'My goodness, there really is a war over here.'"

By his third mission, he had experienced "my ordeal by fire," in which he nearly lost his life. The transformation was complete. "Warfare is ugly. It's not a beautiful thing."

Creating an Air Force

Today we take for granted the existence of an independent United States Air Force—a powerhouse operation that takes a leading role in most of America's offensive and defensive missions. Yet the idea of using aircraft for anything beyond submarine reconnaissance and other behind-the-lines missions was hotly disputed as World War II unfolded.

In the wake of Pearl Harbor, the United States faced the two well-equipped, highly skilled, and disciplined air forces of Germany and Japan, whose pilots flew the best aircraft in the world. Britain's heroic Royal Air Force had shown its defensive ability during the Blitz. What could the United States contribute to the air war in Europe?

Army leaders generally assumed that the role of air power was to support the ground forces; and despite the victories of the Luftwaffe, many expected the conflict in Europe to be mainly a ground war. Military planners, sensing a need for a strong air component, created the Army Air Forces in June 1941. The U.S. Army Air Forces (AAF) won some independence in March 1942 as a co-equal command with Army Ground Forces.

There would be 16 numbered forces in the AAF. One of them became the celebrated aerial champions of the war in Europe: the Eighth Air Force.

Joining Up

Flight captured the imaginations of young Americans. Some had only heard or read about airplanes. Those who grew up on farms had seen crop dusters or had learned to fly them. Even before the war, many a young man dreamed of being a pilot someday.

The Best and the Brightest

Grueling entrance tests for flyers screened out all but the most physically and mentally fit. "We are sending most of the best of our young brains into the air," commented one magazine, *The Saturday Review of Literature.* The popular American writer John Steinbeck noted that air force recruits "are drawn from a cross-section of America, but they are the top part of the cross-section. They are the best we have." Indeed, the Air Forces recruited a higher portion of college-educated men than did the other branches of the armed forces, but recruiters wanted more than brains. They looked for men with mechanical skills, physical toughness, fast reactions, and cool heads under pressure. Entrance tests included questions on mathematics and mechanics, as well as a "mental exam."

A 19-year-old from Mississippi, Alwin Max Juchheim, was birdhunting at college when he heard about Pearl Harbor. "This war will be over before we can get in it," he told his friends. "I'm hitchhikin' down to Jackson; I'm gonna take the exam and see if I can pass it." Juchheim and five other guys made it to Jackson and took the test.

A bomber crew of the Eighth included eight to ten young men from a range of backgrounds and parts of the country. This crew was assembled in the summer of 1944. It included a pilot, a co-pilot, a navigator, a bombardier, and a radio operator. In addition, a top turret gunner, ball turret gunner, one or two waist gunners, and a tail gunner operated at strategic points on the plane, and the top turret gunner was trained as a flight engineer.

Diversity in the Military The Mighty Eighth represented America's diversity in many respects, but not all. Like much of American society in the 1940s, the armed forces were segregated by race. While aircrew service in the Eighth Air Force was limited to white Americans, African Americans served in special services and ordnance. Americans of all ethnic and racial groups served their country and fought for democracy. African American fighter pilots served with distinction in the Fifteenth Air Force in North Africa and Italy.

Close to a million African Americans enlisted or were drafted into the military. At first, they were limited to support positions and did not serve alongside white men in the trenches or in the cockpits. Black leaders pressured the government to change its policy. By late 1942, as the need for soldiers, sailors, and airmen increased, military officials gave in and created separate fighting units for African Americans. The Army Air Force 99th Fighter Squadron, the "Black Eagles," downed more than 110 enemy planes over Italy. The "Tuskegee Airmen" of the Fifteenth Air Force flew more than 1,500 missions in Europe. Their honorable record in combat helped persuade President Harry Truman in 1948 to end segregation in the military.

Fighter pilots of the Tuskegee Airmen are briefed for a mission.

Some 300,000 Mexican Americans were enrolled, most in the Army. They fought in the Pacific, in North Africa, and in the invasion of France in 1944. About 25,000 Native Americans enlisted in the armed services as well.

Japanese Americans, many of whom were imprisoned in remote camps throughout the war, were not accepted into the military until 1943. Thousands came forward to serve. The Japanese American 442nd Regimental Combat unit in Europe became the most decorated military unit in U.S. history.

"It was unheard of, anybody passing it," Juchheim recalls. "They had to have two years of college" and had to score a 90 or above on the examination. "But we took the exam, and I was the only one that passed it." Eventually, all six men made it.

Forming a Crew

One crew of newly trained recruits assigned to a B-17 typifies a cross-section of young American working men: employees of a credit company, an aircraft builder, and a corset-maker; a mechanic, a riveter at an automobile plant, a truck driver, a farmer, an assistant boilermaker, and a baked-goods salesman. Not everyone could be a pilot, navigator, or bombardier. There were many other flying jobs: radio operator/gunners, flight engineer/gunners, and gunners to man the other positions on a bomber.

In *Bombs Away: The Story of a Bomber Team* (1942), Steinbeck characterized the airman as a combination of the rugged "Kentucky hunter and the Western Indian fighter," but with mid-twentieth-century technology, a "Dan'l Boone and Henry Ford."

Why They Joined

With the rise of the Mighty Eighth in Europe, airmen gained an almost celebrity status at home. Famous flyers were called home to make patriotic public appearances to inspire support for the war and to gain new recruits. In fact, some actual Hollywood celebrities put their careers on hold and risked their lives in the skies—actors Jimmy Stewart and Clark Gable among them.

Naturally, some men joined for the glamour. Young, confident, and untested, they couldn't wait to get to Europe for what they thought would be a daring adventure. They witnessed the hero's welcome that awaited those who returned. They imagined their own homecomings and personal achievements. Many of these dreams were never to be. Over 26,000 Eighth Air Force combat crewmen never returned home.

Personal Choices

Mostly, though, men joined the U.S. Army Air Forces for other reasons. "The idea of silver wings, extra pay [for hazardous duty] did not influence me," said one squadron commander, Lieutenant Colonel John Regan of Boise, Idaho. Regan and many others decided to enlist to avoid being drafted and assigned to a particular branch of the military. They preferred to choose the course of their military careers. To some new recruits, flying back from a mission to a cozy barracks with hot meals sounded a lot better than slogging through mud and sleeping in damp trenches, as some ground troops did. The new airmen did not yet know that after each mission, a shocking number of those beds lay empty.

Other men simply heard the call of duty, and responded. Radio operator Ira O'Kennon was simply a poor "country boy" studying at Virginia Polytechnic Institute when he entered the Eighth in 1943. "I was neither aggressive nor ambitious. I did not comprehend the consequences of war, nor did I have any particular vision of anything— pay, career, or comfort. In those days our primary motivator was patriotism."

Frank C. DeCicco, Jr., turned 18 on December 6, 1941, the day before the attack on Pearl Harbor. After finishing high school in the spring of 1942, he enlisted in the Army Air Corps. Why did he want to serve? "I thought that was what you were supposed to do, . . ." says DeCicco, who completed a European tour of duty as a waist gunner. "I was fighting for my family, and for my friends, and for my country."

Fighter Ace. The title meant courage, skill, perseverance, and devotion to country. Ever since World War I, a fighter pilot who downed at least five enemy planes earned the title of flying ace. If he were lucky enough to make it home, an ace could expect a celebrity's welcome.

The U.S. and Britain had many aces in World War II. Some longtime Luftwaffe aces, having flown since 1936 in the Spanish Civil War, as well as on the eastern and western fronts of World War II, had more than 300 victories to their credit. The Luftwaffe's all-time ace, Erich Hartmann, brought down 352 planes on the eastern front in the Soviet Union.

In a 1944 battle near Bremen, Germany, a young fighter squadron leader, Chuck Yeager (later to become famous as the first pilot to fly faster than the speed of sound), counted 22 German fighters in the distance. Yeager led the assault. "[A]ll the airplanes in the sky were spinning and diving in a wild, wide-open dogfight." He downed two German planes in quick succession; then another . . . and another . . . and another. When the fight was over, Chuck Yeager had become America's first "Ace in a Day."

By August 4, 1943, Francis "Gabby" Gabreski had been selected to command a squadron, but didn't have a single victory to his name. He wondered whether he ever would. That day Gabreski downed his first in a total of 28 victories, which would make him America's top-scoring Eighth Air Force ace of World War II.

Into the Unknown

"None of my flight instructors had been in combat, so they had no first-hand experience to pass on, . . ." recalls pilot Max Wooley. Air training took place at bases under the clear skies of Texas, Florida, and other friendly locations.

One trainee in Salt Lake City, Utah had to make a tricky landing on only two of four engines. "That was perfect," said his instructor. "If you can handle jams like this now, combat will be a cinch." Not many combat veterans would agree with the instructor. In fact, the landing was child's play compared with the terror of flying in Europe's constant, blinding rain clouds, seeded with German fighters and deadly anti-aircraft fire.

In the earliest months, new arrivals to the English airfields would be confronted with grim reality: crewmen of the Mighty Eighth had a life expectancy of just 6 to 8 missions. Only 1 in 3 would complete the required 25 missions (later 30, and then 35) and be sent home to the hero's welcome they deserved. The fresh-faced innocents would quickly become hard-bitten men who faced down death day after day. The boastful became humble. The shy learned to take charge—or risk the safety of the crew.

Facing such odds, how did so many men maintain their courage and determination? "[W]e believed in the mission we were on," veteran Carl Mongrue recalls. "We were doing our jobs," says another veteran, Elmer Bendiner. "We were assigned to the particular moment in that time, and we were trying to fulfill it."

Perhaps navigator Jon Schueler summed it up best:
"The men were truly noble."

Eighth Air Force ace Lieutenant General Gerald Johnson

Leaders of the Mighty Eighth

The first combat commander of the Eighth Air Force was Major General Carl A. "Tooey" Spaatz, who was born in 1891 in Pennsylvania. Commissioned in the infantry in 1914, he trained as an Army pilot in 1915. He served in France after the U.S. entered the war and is credited with shooting down three enemy aircraft. He took part in an endurance flight in 1929 when air-to-air refueling was used. When the U.S. entered World War II, he organized air forces to go to the European theater. General Spaatz was commander of the Eighth Air Force from May 5, 1942 until November 30, 1942. After commanding USAAF forces in North Africa, he returned to Great Britain in January, 1944 to become commander of United States Strategic Air Forces in Europe (USSTAAF). After the war, General Spaatz became the first Chief of Staff of the United States Air Force.

Two later commanders of the Eighth Air Force during World War II, General Ira C. Eaker and General James H. Doolittle, happened to have been born in the same year at the close of a century: 1896. But their lives took quite different, but intertwining paths.

General Eaker studied law at Columbia University in New York and journalism at the University of Southern California. He did not serve during World War I, but gained his flying fame afterward. In 1929, he set a world-record 150-hour flight using mid-air refueling, a flight on which he and Spaatz were the pilots. In 1936, he became the first pilot to fly coast-to-coast using instruments only. He took command of the Eighth Bomber Command shortly after its founding, less than three months after Pearl Harbor. He became Commander, Eighth Air Force, in December 1942.

By October 1943, the Mighty Eighth faced mounting losses and received few replacements. Crews flew many heroic missions, but achieved little observable progress in weakening the enemy. Eaker was replaced on January 6, 1944 by an already famous airman, General James "Jimmy" Doolittle.

Doolittle grew up in Nome, Alaska, a wild western mining frontier town that inspired a sense of adventure. He took up amateur boxing and gymnastics. He launched a future in flight by building gliders, then expanded his knowledge by studying engineering. His studies were interrupted by the outbreak of World War I. Doolittle signed up eagerly and became a pilot, although he did not see combat.

General Carl Spaatz (center) commanded the United States Army Air Forces in Europe. General Ira Eaker (fourth from left) and General Jimmy Doolittle (left) led the Eighth Air Force at different times.

After the first world war, he pursued two goals: to learn as much as possible about aviation—aircraft engines, body construction, fuel, and gunnery—and to be an advocate for the Army's use of aircraft. He taught flying, performed spine-tingling acrobatics in air shows, and set records in speed and in cross-country flying. At the same time, he earned a master's degree from the Massachusetts Institute of Technology (MIT). After stints in and out of the military, he was on active duty when Pearl Harbor erupted.

Doolittle went wherever the action was. On April 18, 1942, he led a daring carrier-based bombing raid on Tokyo, Japan. Then, he commanded the Twelfth Air Force in North Africa, the Fifteenth in Italy, and finally the Eighth for its last and most successful years in World War II.

Women in the Cockpit

WANTED: Women ages 21 through 35, at least 5 feet tall, with a high school education or equivalent, American citizenship, and 200 hours of flying experience.

This call from the government in 1942 received 25,000 applications. Only 2,000 of these applicants were accepted. Those who survived rigorous training would become members of an elite group, the Women's Airforce Service Pilots (WASPs).

Before Pearl Harbor, military aircraft were crisscrossing the skies over America and Canada. Skilled male pilots on home duty flew planes wherever they were needed. Bombers fresh from the factory had to be flown to ports for departure to Europe and Asia. Repaired aircraft needed to be flight-tested. Pilots flew planes that dragged targets behind them so trainees could practice shooting them down—a nerve-wracking assignment, to be sure.

Across the Ocean

As the war dragged on, the demand for qualified pilots for the Army Air Forces outpaced supply. Male combat pilots were needed desperately in Europe and the Pacific, and women were not permitted to fly in combat. One skilled flyer, Jacqueline Cochran, saw a solution.

"If women could do the routine of towing targets, or tracking or searchlight missions, or ferrying, whether of a fighter or heavy bomber," Cochran recalled, "it seemed wise to let them do so and release men who had already received combat training, or, of equal importance, release men for other branches of service who would otherwise have to be taken for flying training."

Geography Link   The Great Circle

Most maps show the Earth as a flat plane with straight lines indicating east-west and north-south. Because the world is a globe, this type of flat map can never accurately reflect the relative area and geographical relationships of all the different points on Earth. Some distances are stretched or reduced. The air routes for crossing the North Atlantic illustrate this problem.

Study the map showing the routes that women pilots used to ferry planes from the United States to Britain. Some took a route directly from Newfoundland to a base at Prestwick in northern Britain. Others took a route with stops at airbases in Greenland and Iceland.

If the pilots had chosen what looks like the shortest route on most maps—due east—they would have taken the longest journey of all.

Take a piece of string and a globe. Attach one end of the string to Los Angeles and the other end to London, and pull it tight. This will show the shortest route—the "great circle" route. Plot this route on a flat map. As you can see, the shortest distance between two points may not always look like a straight line.

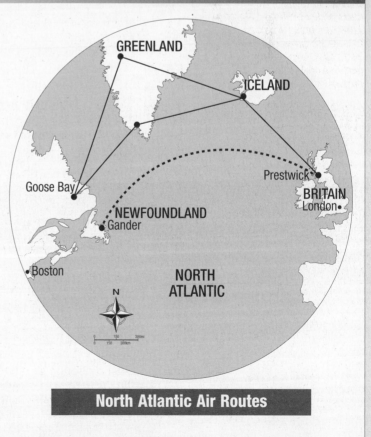

North Atlantic Air Routes

First Lady
Eleanor Roosevelt

"We are in a war and we need to fight it with all our ability and every weapon possible. WOMEN PILOTS, in this particular case, are a weapon waiting to be used."

—First Lady Eleanor Roosevelt, 1942

To fill the void, Cochran and another superb and determined pilot, Nancy Harkness Love, each petitioned the government separately to create a women's air corps.

"England had already found use for about all of their own [qualified women pilots] and 25 of our American women pilots," Cochran pointed out, "and Russia, according to general information, was using women pilots even in combat and extensively in routine flying."

Plenty of skepticism greeted the idea, but it received crucial support from the First Lady, who said, "This is not a time when women should be patient. We are in a war and we need to fight it with all our ability and every weapon possible. WOMEN PILOTS, in this particular case, are a weapon waiting to be used."

Cochran and Love eventually received permission to create separate ferrying and training programs for women. In 1943, those programs merged to become the Women's Airforce Service Pilots.

The WASPs

According to Cochran, the organization had three goals: "(1) to see if women could serve as military pilots and if so, to form the nucleus of an organization that could be rapidly expanded; (2) to release male pilots for combat; (3) to decrease the Air Forces' total demands on the cream of the manpower pool."

The WASPs never lacked for applicants.

"There were always several hundred applicants on this waiting list," said Cochran. "The selection was entirely a matter of choosing clean-cut, stable-appearing young girls of the proper ages, educational background, and height, who could show the required number of flying hours properly noted and certified in a log book." In August 1944, the required minimum height was raised to 64 inches.

Clearly, putting women in the cockpit was an experiment. "How women pilots would prove out as a whole in relation to fatigue, strain, emergencies, and in connection with physiology peculiar to their sex, were largely unknown factors for determination," Cochran reported.

A Record of Accomplishment

In fact, women performed with great ability. They were expected to pass the same rigorous AAF tests that the men did. In their 23 weeks of training in Sweetwater, Texas, they practiced cross-country, instrument, and night flying—even acrobatics. "[E]mphasis was placed on developing good operational pilots, rather than 'hot' pilots. . . . Stunts or 'headline' flying was consequently discouraged. The WASPs were continually cautioned to leave the glamour and glory for their brother pilots who were over the front lines, and that the WASP operation was a routine group endeavor."

Discipline was tight. The job demanded commitment. No dating your instructor. Or your student—women also taught male trainees how to strafe and bomb.

During the course of the war, women flew every type of plane in the U.S. military. They ferried 18,652 planes, and earned an excellent safety record.

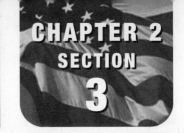

Bombers

Two of the Army's heavy bombers, the B-17 and B-24, were American mainstays in the air war over Europe. These monster machines had been designed and manufactured before the United States went to war. A few true believers knew from the start that these aircraft could change the course of the war—and of future wars. Yet the doubters persisted. Indeed, Britain and Germany continued to favor lighter, more maneuverable aircraft throughout the war.

These aircraft would have to prove their worth. A new B-17 cost $250,000, a giant sum at the time. In the end, they proved priceless.

The B-17 Flying Fortress

"The B-17 was an absolutely awesome airplane to fly in formation," recalls Craig Harris. Unveiled in 1935, Boeing's new so-called "heavy bomber," weighing in at 35,000 pounds, sported the high technology of its day. It had four engines instead of two, and five gunner's stations, or turrets. Later improvements allowed the aircraft to climb to 35,000 feet and travel up to 287 miles an hour.

Offensively and defensively, the B-17 was armed to the teeth. It stowed three tons of bombs in its bomb bays, with room for more beneath the wings, although this option was rarely used. For protection, it boasted twelve .50-caliber machine guns. One .30 caliber gun was included at first but later removed. When flown in the formation of a box, the Flying Fortresses could inflict serious damage on attacking fighters. Most of the nearly 13,000 B-17s built before and during the war years served ably in Europe.

B-17 Flying Fortress

The B-24 Liberator

In January 1939, with war in Europe looming, Army commanders put out a call for a successor to the B-17. Their wish list included a range of 3,000 miles, a bomb load of 2,500 pounds, and a maximum altitude of 35,000 feet—about 6.6 miles up. And they wanted it by the end of the year. On December 29, 1939, Consolidated Aircraft unveiled a new B-24, called "Liberator."

The Army didn't get exactly what it wanted, but it got a very good bomber. The Liberator was a high-altitude bomber with a range of nearly 1,600 miles—40 percent farther than the B-17 and critical to bombing sites deep within Germany; a top speed of 295 miles an hour; and a maximum altitude of about 28,000 feet. After some adjustments, it could hold a payload of nearly 13,000 pounds, although a typical bomb load was 6,000 pounds so the plane could reach combat service altitudes. B-24s typically flew at an altitude of 24,000 feet or less.

The Liberator at War

To fly the Liberator, however, was an exhausting experience. Simply put, it didn't have power steering, power brakes, or power rudders. "I don't think there's a person alive that could fly a formation of B-24s for 10, 12, or 13 hours" without specific B-24 training, recalled George McGovern, a future U.S. senator and presidential candidate.

American companies built some 19,000 B-24s, more than any other aircraft. The British and French air corps placed orders for them, but before the planes could be delivered, France fell captive to the Germans.

B-24 Liberator bombers of the Second Air Division, identified by their oval tails, carried the war to the enemy in both the Mighty Eighth and the Fifteenth Air Forces. Liberators made up the forces that attacked the German-held oil fields in Romania.

Fighters

The fighter fought its first battles in Washington, D.C. The top AAF commanders had come from bomber groups or were strong backers of the bomber as a tool of war. The fighter plane—fast, nimble, and well-armed; descended from the tradition of the World War I dogfighters—had a tough time getting respect. The huge, rugged, long-distance bombers, although not yet battle-tested, had a reputation for being nearly invincible. Why, then, would they need protection from fighter escorts?

As the Army Air Forces would tragically discover, German fighters and anti-aircraft guns could chew up even the Flying Fortress and send them spiraling to the ground. The early Flying Fortresses turned out to be quite at risk, lacking protective armor and adequate firepower. Increasingly, the value of fighter aircraft as escorts and, later, as attack planes, became clear.

American Fighters

The fighters of World War II—American, British, German, and Japanese— topped 400 miles an hour and reached dizzying heights of over 33,000 feet. A handful of these remarkable machines, Allied and Axis, earned enormous fame: the British Hurricane and Spitfire; the German Messerschmitt and Focke-Wulf; the Japanese Zero; and two American champions, the Thunderbolt and Mustang.

Speedy at all altitudes, the turbocharged P-38 "Lightning" became the first American fighter to escort Eighth Air Force bombers. But the need for ever more speed and distance led to the development of the P-47 "Thunderbolt." A well-named companion and then successor to the Lightning, the Thunderbolt became the workhorse fighter of World War II, flying in Europe and the Pacific. The P-47 could serve as a fighter-bomber. It could dive at 500 miles an hour and it could take punishment from the enemy and keep on fighting.

P-38/F-5 fighter plane

The P-51 Mustang had a longer range than the earlier P-38 and P-47 fighters, and together with the new generation of P-38s and P-47s, the P-51 extended escort protection for bombers far into German airspace.

Extending the Range of Fighters

With the Thunderbolt, American engineers still had not solved the problem of distance. As the war progressed, the Allies needed bombers to take the war to the enemy—that is, to bomb targets deep inside Germany. American bombers could make the trip, but their fighter escorts could barely cross the German border when they would have to turn back, with just enough fuel, they hoped, to get back home. As they dropped away, frustrated fighter pilots saw German planes in the distance, waiting to bounce the bombers as soon as they lost their protection.

After many modifications, including the addition of a Rolls Royce-built engine, the new P-51 "Mustang" overcame the distance factor, with a tactical radius (with two wing tanks) of about 750 miles. Fitting wing tanks to the P-47 Thunderbolt increased that fighter's tactical radius to 475 miles. Fighter escorts of bombers were greatly facilitated by acquisition of bases on the European continent in 1944. Thunderbolts operating from these forward bases caused great destruction of enemy front line positions and rail transportation.

Besides providing bomber protection, the Mustang was a warrior. Its pilots, many of whom once flew P-47s, downed nearly 5,000 enemy planes. Now America's Fortresses and Liberators could advance deep into Germany—with mighty bodyguards at their side.

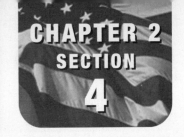

The Home Team

Civilians at War

Americans went to war by the hundreds, then by the thousands, then by the millions—without ever leaving home. They never looked the enemy in the eye; they fired no shots.

These heroes received no parades. Yet without them, America's war effort would have ground to a halt.

They were the women and men on the "home front." They kept the tanks and ships and guns coming; built the Flying Fortresses and the Mustangs; kept the soldiers in warm socks and blankets. They showed up for work and worked hard, even the brokenhearted who had just lost a son or a sweetheart.

American factories produced 300,000 airplanes during the war, far more than Germany or Britain were capable of manufacturing.

America's Wartime Economy

The United States proved that there is power in numbers. These figures help tell the story:

- During World War II, more than 10 million Americans served in the military.

- About 3.5 million women signed up for factory jobs to replace the men who served at the front lines; the majority had never worked outside the home before.

- In just four years, the United States produced some 300,000 airplanes, 100,000 tanks and self-propelled guns, 71,000 naval ships, 5,500 cargo vessels, 2.5 million trucks, and 44 billion rounds of small-arms ammunition.

Science Link   A New Fabric for Wartime

In 1928, a group of chemists huddled in laboratories in Delaware began a super-secret project that revolutionized the materials we wear and use today. This revolution arrived just in time to make its mark on World War II.

On a remarkable day in 1930, a researcher pulled a glass rod out of a hot, soupy substance made from carbon and alcohol. The stuff, when drawn out into the air, formed a flexible fiber-like strand. Stretched to four times its length, the fiber became extremely strong. The discovery led to the creation, in 1938, of the first truly human-made fiber. It was called nylon.

The research team wanted to explore what new materials could be made by combining polymers—large molecules in a chain-like formation. Polymers could be used to create strong, silky fibers for nylon fabric and other plastics. It began a whole new era of synthetics.

Nylon first hit the market as women's hosiery, replacing expensive silk stockings. "Nylons" were such a fashion rage that they sold out quickly. With the onset of war, the government bought up supplies of the durable nylon for use in making parachutes, tents, ropes, and cords, and even tires for B-29 bombers. As quickly as nylons had appeared on store shelves, they were taken off the market—a casualty of the war effort.

Question: How is nylon an example of science influencing industry?

Seemingly overnight, the merciless, unyielding economic Depression of the 1930s gave way to an economy in full swing. From deep unemployment to full employment, the jobs were there for anyone willing and able. America's industrial production soared, and all that held it back were shortages of raw materials and labor. The nation's mighty machinery switched gears, making airplanes instead of cars, bombs instead of clocks, and parachutes instead of jackets.

Uncle Sam Takes Control

This miraculous transformation began immediately after Pearl Harbor. It took place under the strong arm of the federal government. A new federal agency, the War Production Board, swung into action to coordinate the efforts of U.S. industries. The board had sweeping powers to decide the basic economic questions of what to produce and how much to produce. It set levels for prices and wages. It could require manufacturers to produce aircraft engines instead of, say, refrigerators. The board also banned the production of goods it judged unnecessary, including bicycles, waffle irons, coat hangers, and the worst offender of all: automobiles. The steel, glass, rubber, and gasoline needed to build and run an automobile was diverted to serve new fleets of tanks, jeeps, ships, and planes.

Such deep government involvement in America's free enterprise economy had never occurred before and has not since. Business leaders, accustomed to running their companies as they wished, chafed at this governmental interference, but federal decisionmakers had the last word. The government could deny essential raw materials to an uncooperative manufacturer, saying that the materials were needed for wartime use. However, the government offered sweet rewards for companies that made the weapons of war. Government contracts included healthy profits for them as a motivation to do their best.

In a capitalist country, if you are going to war, "you have to let business make money out of the process, or business won't work," Secretary of War Henry L. Stimson wrote in his diary. Still, plenty of businesses patriotically offered their services to aid the war effort.

American Industry Responds

Before Pearl Harbor, Ford Motor Company had already begun defense operations in its new facility outside Detroit—the world's largest aircraft manufacturing plant at Willow Run, Michigan (about a quarter-mile wide and a half-mile long). It built one B-24 Liberator every hour. Soon after Pearl Harbor, the government placed orders for $6 billion in aircraft and equipment.

Orders from Uncle Sam were not always easy to fill. A Ford automobile contained only about 15,000 parts. On the other hand, each B-24 Liberator had about 100,000 parts. Furthermore, aircraft engineers continually improved their designs, requiring factory assembly lines to retool their machines to produce the new models. Over the course of the war, these modifications increased the top speed of a B-17 Flying Fortress from 256 miles per hour to 287 and its maximum range improved from about 1,300 miles to 2,000.

Women package spare engine parts on an assembly line while a few men work on the sidelines.

Soldiers Without Uniforms

In the aircraft industry alone, the need for workers soared from about 100,000 in 1940 to more than 2 million at the height of production. The dramatic increase in the aircraft workforce was matched in other important industries, including shipbuilding and armaments production. Until the war, most manufacturers did not employ women in factories. World War II forever challenged the belief that women were incapable of hard, skilled manual labor.

At first some companies still refused to hire women and minorities. But as the demand for labor shot up, women, African Americans, teenagers, and prison inmates wound up on assembly lines. Older citizens went to work at home. The aim was for any able American to take a job that would free up a man for military duty.

Rosie the Riveter

Women took—and excelled at—jobs that were difficult and exhausting. One petite 19-year-old from Mississippi, Vera Anderson, gained nationwide fame as the undisputed women's welding champion. The strength and determination of women laborers came to be symbolized by the fictional character "Rosie the Riveter." Rosie the Riveter appeared on posters everywhere: her hair tucked in a red bandana, rolling up a sleeve of her coveralls to reveal the muscular arm of a bodybuilder.

Indeed, it took Rosie-like strength and endurance to rivet even a medium-sized bomber such as the B-25, held together by some 150,000 rivets. A worker at the Philadelphia Navy Yard remembered the challenge of assembling a Flying Fortress. "You had to grip your [rivet] gun very tightly as you worked." said Helen Kosierowski, who worked the midnight-to-8 A.M. shift at the Philadelphia Navy Yard riveting together B-29s. "My partner and I had to stand way up high on a plank to rivet the tail section. When we started the rivet gun, the whole plane shook. If the gun got away from you, it would fly all over the place, making everyone take cover until someone shut it down."

Dangerous Work

Civilian workers earned the name "soldiers without uniforms." Many jobs were extremely dangerous, such as manufacturing and handling live bombs and ammunition. Former factory worker Estrella Montgomery recalls a Thanksgiving Day on which she had to work, putting fuses into bombs.

"During our shift, one worker let a bomb slip through her hands—*and its nose fuse was in place!*" It landed on the worker's shoe instead of on the concrete floor. "Had that bomb hit on its nose, the building and most of the entire Ammunition Depot surrounding it probably would have gone up in a gigantic explosion!"

The government asked for the help of all factory workers in not divulging technology secrets to possible spies. Workers heeded the posters that warned: "Loose Lips Sink Ships."

Likewise, hard work saved lives. No one knew that better than sailor Elgin Staples. When his ship was sunk in the Pacific, he was washed overboard. Staples later discovered that the life belt that saved his life had been inspected and stamped back in his hometown of Akron, Ohio—by his mother.

As men went to the front lines to fight, American women went to work by the millions in war factories.

Sacrificing for War

At the news that America was under attack, women, like men, lined up at recruiting stations to enlist in the service. Many were young and single, willing to put their lives on hold in sacrifice to their country. More than 200,000 women were on active military duty during the war, many of them in the United States. Women did not operate guns in combat, but skilled shooters became gunnery instructors for new male recruits. Besides becoming pilots in the WASPs and other military organizations, enlisted women became telegraph operators, map readers, air traffic controllers, plumbers, electricians, photographers, and aircraft engine mechanics.

In civilian roles, those not working in factories found other ways to contribute. Everyone from kids to grandmothers volunteered for the Red Cross, church groups, and countless charity groups. From celebrities to local talent, entertainers traveled the United States and overseas to brighten the dark days for lonely, homesick troops.

Rationing and Recycling

The lives of virtually every American changed unimaginably from the start of the war. The Roosevelt administration began to *ration*—to allow only limited purchases of—everyday products from butter and sugar to gasoline. A gas ration of three gallons per week per family allowed them to travel only about 45 miles in the heavy automobiles of the time. People began to get around on foot, by bicycle, or by bus.

Even these solutions caused new problems. Long walks to work and shopping wore out shoes, but civilians were limited to only two pairs a year. A few enterprising civilians brought old electric and steam-powered cars out of storage.

Rationing During World War II, important resources, including food, gasoline, heating oil, and clothing, were needed for the servicemen fighting in the war. The war at sea cut America off from some vital sources of imported goods, like rubber, and limited shipping space for importing others. Americans on the home front were limited to a certain amount per person of these goods.

Rationed foods included:

- Sugar
- Coffee
- Meat
- Milk
- Butter
- Cheese
- Processed foods

Sugar was rationed for the longest period of time—from 1942 until 1947, almost two years after the war had ended. At its height, 91% of the population had sugar ration cards.

Individuals were given ration books with a certain number of points they could use each week for rationed goods. The point system was separate from pricing. A shopper needed to have enough cash and enough points to buy a cut of meat or bag of sugar at the store.

Cars were not manufactured during the war. Rubber for tires was scarce, and gasoline was limited to three gallons a week for all but those with the most essential travel needs. The rationing system was confusing and often frustrating, but it was a necessary sacrifice to keep the war effort going.

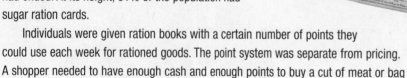

The nation's farm production was needed to feed the men in battle. So the government encouraged families to plant their own "victory gardens," as in World War I, to supplement the food supply. Two years after Pearl Harbor, 20 million victory gardens were producing one third of America's fresh vegetables.

The nation also embarked on the most massive recycling operation in history. Facing an unrelenting demand for metal, the government urged its citizens to donate or collect scrap metal for bombs and other uses. People collected everything from pots and pans to old car parts. Women turned in their silk and nylon stockings, which were turned into gunpowder bags and parachutes. Children collected milkweed pods, with white fluff inside that could be dried and used to stuff life jackets. They stomped on tin cans to flatten them for recycling. In 1942, the military needed every scrap of rubber available to deal with a desperate shortage. A single B-17 contained about 1,000 pounds of rubber. Americans creatively patched and repatched their old car and bicycle tires throughout the war or put their cars up on blocks until the end of rationing.

Protecting the Homeland

Along the country's coastlines, air raid lookouts scanned the skies round the clock to watch for enemy planes. Coastal cities mounted anti-aircraft guns atop high buildings in case of attack. Blackouts and painted auto headlights were routinely used as far from the coast as Oklahoma.

Air raid drills became a part of life in some parts of the United States, just as they had in Britain. Carolyn Costello Schiro remembers the required blackouts:

"Our house was up on a hill, and from the sun porch that ran across the back we could see all of San Francisco below. I would run there as soon as the sirens began, and watch as each light went out all over the city until all I could see was a sheet of blackness. When the 'all clear' sounded, I'd run there again to watch the city come back to life." Neighborhood volunteer wardens dashed from their homes when the air raid sirens sounded, keeping people off the streets and knocking on the doors of any home where the lights were still on.

Everyone Pitches In

Americans showed their commitment to the war effort in large and small ways. One eight-year-old boy, Jerald Oldroyd, went to school once a week with money to buy savings stamps, which helped fund the war effort. He could buy a stamp for 10 cents. Or he could buy two candy bars, or a soft drink. "I had a choice—candy or stamps," Jerald said. "It wasn't a hard choice to make."

> *Think about how difficult* it would feel to be a telegram messenger who went to two or three homes a day to deliver this horrible news from the government: "We regret to inform you that your son John was killed in action . . ." A gold star hung in the windows of homes of the war dead. Their parents, brothers and sisters, and newly widowed young wives had made the ultimate sacrifice at home.

Character Values

Tolerance

Civilians were safe from enemy attack, but their lives were by no means easy. The conveniences Americans take for granted today—and before the war— could not be sustained. Civilians demonstrated the extent of their tolerance when their favorite foods vanished from shelves, clothes faded and grew ragged, and shoes wore thin. Whining was unacceptable—don't you know there's a war on?

Buttons on their collars identify these women as Red Cross volunteers.

Should the Army Air Forces develop the means to conduct strategic bombing?

During World War I, airplanes were used primarily to scout out enemy positions and to destroy enemy aircraft. However, there were other uses for airplanes during war that did not directly involve ground troops. During World War I, German raids on Britain killed or wounded about 2,000 people, primarily civilians. The German attacks on Britain were among the first strategic bomber raids.

Brigadier-General Billy Mitchell, a strong advocate of air power in the United States during the 1920s, defined strategic bombing as "strik[ing] directly at centers of production, means of transportation, agricultural areas, ports and shipping. . . ." By doing so, "they will destroy the means of making war."

> *"They will destroy the means of making war."*
>
> —*Brigadier-General Billy Mitchell on strategic bombers*

Strategic bombing moved beyond front line war zones and targeted non-military areas of enemy countries. The purpose of strategic bombing was to destroy the enemy country's ability to produce war goods and lower morale.

Strategic bombing was a controversial subject. Many people felt that attacking civilians was uncivilized behavior, even in wartime. Civilians, especially women and children, were noncombatants—they did not fight and were not considered part of the war. Many people protested after German bombers destroyed the Spanish town of Guernica. War, no matter how destructive, was understood to follow certain rules of behavior. Strategic bombing threatened to overturn those rules by exposing noncombatants to attack.

However, the rules of war were changing. The total wars of the 20th century involved every citizen. In the United States during World War II, the civilian workforce was critical to the production of war supplies. The Allies' greater capacity to produce war supplies enabled them to triumph over the Axis.

The result hoped for in strategic bombing was that it could end wars more quickly than traditional combat. No country wanted to re-create the trench warfare of World War I, with its unending deadly struggles for small territorial gains. If strategic bombing would disrupt the flow of supplies to the front, and destroy the enemy's will to wage war, the army would be forced to surrender.

British Air Marshal Arthur T. Harris, Commander of Royal Air Force Bomber Command, took this argument a step further. He argued that by

> *"We thought of air warfare in 1938 rather as people think of nuclear warfare today."*
>
> —*British Prime Minster Harold MacMillan*

destroying the homes of workers in industrial cities—not necessarily taking any lives—strategic bombing could bring factories to a halt and create a housing and refugee problem too tough for the enemy to resolve. Low morale among civilians would pressure enemy leaders to surrender. Harris's viewpoint was more extreme than what American leaders believed.

The ultimate goal of strategic bombing was the dream that said the use of strategic bombers would eliminate war on the ground, and eventually, war itself.

The aftermath of German bombing in York, England.

After the attack on Guernica, people around the world "thought of air warfare in 1938 rather as people think of nuclear warfare today," British Prime Minister Harold MacMillan remembered. People hoped that investing in strategic bombers would prevent war much the same way that nuclear arsenals would deter war a generation later. The threat of bomber attacks would be so terrifying that no nation would be willing to start a war.

The deciding factor for the U.S. Army Air Corps to accelerate development and production of long-range bombers was the conquest of France in June 1940. The Luftwaffe provided crucial support in the German conquest of the Netherlands, Belgium, and France. The very threat of strategic bombing in Utrecht and Rotterdam caused the beleaguered Dutch to surrender. Bombing by the Luftwaffe also nearly prevented Allied troops from escaping annihilation at Dunkirk. With the situation in Europe so desperate, the United States realized that it needed every possible weapon available to counter the threat. Money was provided to develop and build long-range bombers.

Making a Decision

Use the following steps below to evaluate the decision by the United States to carry out strategic bombing against Germany in World War II. As you read each step, think of the important issues raised by the debate over strategic bombing.

◆ **Identify the problem and express it clearly.** First, determine whether a decision is needed; then clarify what needs to be decided. What is the issue you want to resolve or the goal you want to achieve? Reread the arguments presented in this selection and describe the two opposing viewpoints in this debate in your own words.

◆ **Gather Information.** Find out facts about the issue. Be sure that your sources are reliable. List one fact and

one opinion for each side in the debate over investing in bombers for strategic bombing.

◆ **Identify options.** Be sure to consider all the ways an issue might be handled. Stating the options clearly will help you decide. Describe the options faced by the Allies in this debate.

◆ **Predicting consequences.** Identify the pros and cons of each choice. List one advantage and one disadvantage of each option.

◆ **Make a decision.** Evaluate your options; choose the one with the most acceptable consequences. Describe the choice made by the Allies with respect to strategic bombing and explain why this was considered the best choice overall.

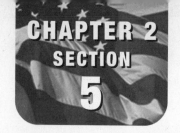

CHAPTER 2
SECTION
5

The First Missions

A Rough Start

Bombing the enemy in broad daylight? "Precision" bombing at high altitudes? How precisely can you aim a bomb from four miles up, where you can't tell the difference between a turtle and a tank? To put it more accurately, you can barely see the large warehouses and rail yards that are your prime bombing targets.

British pilots said the Americans were nuts.

The Royal Air Force (RAF) had already tried daytime bombing and been badly stung with heavy losses. After defeating the Nazis in the Battle of Britain, the British sought revenge on Germany. The United States sent over about 20 B-17 bombers for the British in the spring of 1941. In combat, these American bombers did not perform well for the RAF. Bombs missed their targets. Guns froze. Missions had to be aborted.

"The Brits flew too high!" the Americans protested. Instead of bombing at around 20,000 feet as intended, the RAF bombed from 30,000 feet and above, which made it impossible to hit the targets. Furthermore, the lack of oxygen and extreme cold at these high altitudes posed special problems.

America stood by its plan. High-altitude, daytime, precision bombing would win the day, they declared.

Norden Bombsight

America's Strategy: Daytime Bombing

The commander of the Eighth Air Force, General Ira Eaker, believed in the daytime bombing strategy and had pushed for it vigorously within the Army Air Forces (AAF). American strategists noted that the RAF's "area bombing"—dumping a large amount of bombs in a broad circle around the target in hopes that some of the bombs would hit it—caused a great deal of damage outside the target zone.

The technique ran the risk of killing high numbers of civilians who lived near military or industrial sites. Some strategists in both America and Britain saw that as a necessary evil of war. People who supplied the labor to produce Germany's arms should be targets along with the buildings, according to this view. AAF leaders firmly rejected this argument.

Science Link   The Norden Bombsight

It had "sight" but could not see. It bombed, but was not a bombardier. It flew B-17s, but was not a pilot. And it was so top secret that airmen had to take an oath to defend it with their lives.

The Norden bombsight marked a technological advance in aviation warfare. Invented in the 1920s by American engineer Carl Norden, the bombsight was first used by the Navy and adapted by the Army Air Forces for use in World War II.

The complex instrument performed a remarkable set of tasks: As a bomber approached its target, the Norden system actually took control of the aircraft. The automatic pilot used a device called a *gyroscope* to hold the plane steady, because a change in altitude or air speed could cause the bombs to veer off

course. The bombardier looked through a built-in telescope and kept it fixed on the target. At the right moment, the bombsight, using a system of more than 2,000 gears and other parts, opened the bomb bay doors and released the payload. Then it returned control of the aircraft to the pilots.

Estimates of the bombsight's accuracy vary widely, but the technology did aid the Eighth Air Force's bold plan for high-altitude daytime bombing. The AAF claimed the device could drop a bomb within a 100-foot circle from an altitude of about four miles. Bombardiers liked to say that the Norden bombsight could "put a bomb in a pickle barrel from 20,000 feet."

Question: Why did bombing accuracy decrease when planes flew at high altitudes?

48

A Joint Plan

The AAF and the RAF agreed in 1943 at the Casablanca Conference that bombing would shorten the war and save many lives, military and civilian. Despite disagreements about techniques, they worked together to create a bombing strategy: The RAF would bomb German cities at night, hoping to spread fear and crush the German people's appetite for war. The Mighty Eighth would use daytime precision bombing to target important industrial and military sites.

Furthermore, American bombers would fly into Germany without the protection of fighter escorts, which could fly for only a limited distance in 1942. Eaker and other leaders were counting on the Flying Fortresses and Liberators to fly high enough, fast enough, and with enough ammunition and gunners, to ward off any attackers.

Then what about accuracy? An RAF study showed that its nighttime area bombing usually missed the targets by a mile. In fact, sometimes five miles or more! The British adapted their radar systems to improve accuracy, but with little success.

The United States hoped to do better. The AAF's confidence in a daytime bombing plan rested partly on a new technology known only to the Americans: the Norden bombsight. The revolutionary bombsight would solve the problem of precision bombing at high altitudes, its supporters predicted. It would become a symbol of American innovation, its "can do" spirit.

Rouen

The first major test of U.S. daytime bombing took place in one of the cultural treasures of Europe: Rouen, in Nazi-occupied France. The ancient port city along the Seine River was nicknamed "museum city" because of its historic cathedrals and other cultural landmarks. The Nazis prized Rouen for its strategic deep-water ports, a stone's throw away from the English Channel and about 90 miles northwest of the French capital, Paris. The Allies targeted Rouen because of its vast rail yards, where war supplies were shuttled far and wide across conquered lands.

On August 17, 1942, the commander of the Eighth Bomber Command, Gen. Ira Eaker, prepared to fly in the attack in his bomber, the *Yankee Doodle*. "I don't want any American mothers to think I'd send their boys someplace where I'd be afraid to go myself," Eaker said.

The mission originated in England, where the Eighth Air Force would eventually operate more than 60 airfields. American pilots had flown borrowed planes on mixed British-American missions since June. Rouen would be the first all-American mission for the Eighth.

"It was cause for celebration, for finally we were gonna get it done or fail desperately in trying as many, especially in the RAF Bomber Command, predicted," explained Walt Kelly, a 23-year-old volunteer from Pennsylvania. "We just wanted to be let loose to punish Hitler and the Luftwaffe."

On the short mission to Rouen, four squadrons of RAF Spitfire fighters escorted 12 B-17 Flying Fortresses piloted by the men of the Ninety-Seventh Bomb Group. From an altitude of 25,000 feet, they dropped more than 18 tons of bombs on freight yards and related buildings in the strategic city. Fifty percent of the bombs hit their targets—a very high success rate.

By the standards of later missions, the Rouen mission was minor. In fact, the Germans repaired the damage fairly quickly. Yet the mission sent a message: Occupied Europe had now come under attack by the United States. From the Rouen mission in 1942, to the present day, air power would gradually become America's main weapon of warfare. That is the long-term significance of the bombing of Rouen.

Grafton Underwood served as the base for the first all-American air attack on a German target. Compare this map to the map of Europe on p. 78.

What were two reasons why Rouen was chosen as the Eighth's target in summer 1942, instead of a city in Germany?

Life at 25,000 Feet

No war movie, no video game, can imitate the experiences of the men of the Mighty Eighth. Real bullets, real enemies, frostbitten toes—with real courage they not only faced these dangers. They had to perform at their very best, on every mission.

Even without the hot breath of enemy fighters at their backs, Eighth airmen battled to stay alive and to keep their planes in the air. The lives they lived above the clouds for hours each day were, at best, uncomfortable and, at worst, perilous. The best way to understand the experience is to hear it from those who lived to tell their stories.

"Physically, the B-17 was not made for rider comfort. . . . It was noisy, drafty, lots of vibration . . ." says co-pilot Craig Harris. "In combat . . . we flew at anywhere from 23,000 to 26,000 feet. . . . At those altitudes, one finds environmentally, a very hostile place; it's cold. Minus 30 degrees Fahrenheit was considered a warm day. We flew several missions where it was 70 [degrees] below."

That's the typical winter climate at the frozen interior of Antarctica.

> ## "[T]he temperatures at 30,000 to 32,000 feet were 40 to 70 degrees below zero."
>
> —*Bill Flemming*

Preparing for the Cold

"We had to dress for the cold," Harris remembers. "We did have electric flying suits. I wore mine; I wore it as an extra set of long johns. I just wore it for the layered protection; I never plugged it in. It occurred to me if I ever had to leave the airplane, I'd have to unplug; that's one thing that would tie me to the airplane that had to be undone. Also, I wouldn't have the electricity from the airplane [if the plane had mechanical failure or was hit], so I wouldn't have a heated suit anyway. So I did not depend on the electric suit for my warmth.

I had lunch today with a man who did depend on his electric suit and his electric boots. He lost power and didn't know it—and his feet froze. He is permanently

The airman's protection at 25,000 feet included a helmet, goggles, an oxygen mask, and warm socks.

Why was the oxygen mask necessary?

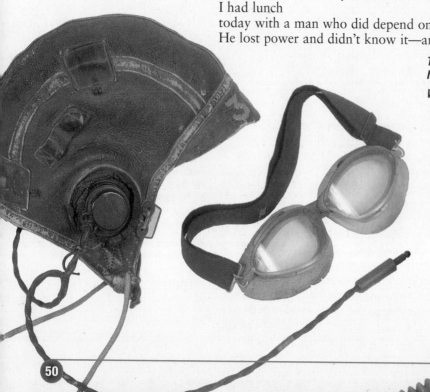

disabled today. . . ."

From the exposed position of the gunner's turret, Bill Flemming battled the cold from a different perspective:

"[T]he temperatures at 30,000 to 32,000 feet were 40 to 70 degrees below zero. We had to dress very heavily. I wore long underwear, and a uniform shirt and pants, an electric suit over that, plus a fur-lined flying suit on top of it. On my feet I wore silk stockings, wool stockings, electric [heated] shoes, and fur-lined flying boots. My hands had silk gloves, wool gloves, electric gloves, and the fur-lined flying mitts.

"You could barely move a finger," Flemming recalls, "and you always left one free to work the trigger of the machine gun. We didn't dare unplug the electric suits, which were connected to the [airplane's] battery system. Without heat you would freeze to death in a matter of minutes. . . ."

A formation of B-17 bombers flies out on a mission.

Oxygen

In fact, high-altitude flying was one giant experiment, and the equipment made to keep the men alive occasionally failed. "The older oxygen masks were very bad," Craig Harris says. The moisture in the men's breath would collect in the mask and freeze, and some men died because of the lack of oxygen. "You'd have to keep moving [the masks] to break up the ice . . ."

"You did not dare fly while you had a cold," Flemming recalls. If you did, your oxygen mask "would freeze with ice and cut off your oxygen."

Damage to the main oxygen could also cause death. "We did carry what we call 'walk around' bottles, and [they] have saved many a man . . ." says Harris. "Oxygen was always on our minds. . . ."

"One of the things we did regularly was to keep in touch with each other on the interphone . . . just to make sure some guy was not on the edge of hypoxia [lack of oxygen]. One of the insidious things about oxygen loss at [high] altitude is that you don't realize it's happening. Everything's rosy; you're happy; you don't even know why you were complaining about being on the mission. Everything is so nice. Next thing you know, if you let that go too far, you're dead."

The Challenges of the Bomber

The Flying Fortress had all the comforts and safety features you would expect of a stone fortress in the sky. "The airplanes were drafty, and some of the waist [mid-section] windows were actually open," says Harris. "When the bomb bay doors were opened, that airplane got hard to fly because it was like having a sea anchor overboard. You had a big hole open to the sky; a lot of air came and went, and it was noisy and it was just very difficult to fly.

"Unfortunately, on the bomb run, you do most of the run with the doors open, and that was part of being a good formation pilot—learning to fly that airplane with the altered flight characteristics it had with the doors hanging down. . . . A B-17 with the doors open is not a fun plane to fly, especially in formation, in which we were expected to fly."

Open doors and windows meant that the plane was unpressurized. At high altitude, the atmosphere in an unpressurized cabin required the passengers to have oxygen. It also could cause painful damage to the ears—and even cause crewmen to pass out—if there were a sudden, swift change in altitude.

Character Values

Respect for the Environment

Five miles up in the air, fighting frigid air and difficult weather, the airmen of the Mighty Eighth learned respect for the environment. An unexpected storm could damage a plane as easily as a Luftwaffe fighter; an unprotected airman could lose flesh to the cold and even die from lack of oxygen.

Loyalty

The unpressurized, rugged aircraft of World War II made flying conditions hazardous even without enemy fire. Survival in the air depended upon group cohesion, loyalty to each other. Crew members kept each other's safety and well-being in mind for the greater good of the crew. Co-pilot Ralph Golubock's awareness and quick thinking when his pilot experienced vertigo enabled an entire crew to return safely to base.

Vertigo

Fighter aircraft, light and mobile, were built to be highly maneuverable, to climb and dive like a bird. These wild rides subjected some pilots to airsickness and to a worse danger, *vertigo,* an overwhelming sensation of dizziness and disorientation. While the heavy bombers lacked the maneuverability of fighters, bomber crews still were subject to attacks of vertigo. It was serious, and it could force a pilot to have to give up his job.

Co-pilot Ralph Golubock saw the effects of vertigo first-hand while flying a mission over occupied Europe. "About 10 minutes into our climb, I began to feel that something was wrong." Golubock looked at the instrument readings to determine what was happening to his plane. "We were headed down into a steep spiral to the left and our air speed had increased to about 200 miles per hour. If we continued in this position, we would surely crash in a few seconds."

Golubock tapped the pilot on the shoulder. No response. "By this time the engineer was also alarmed and screamed for me to take over. I grabbed the yoke, while the engineer pulled [the pilot's] hands off. I was able to gradually level the airplane and started into a normal climb. [The pilot] then took over control. . . . Vertigo is one of the reasons that the Air Force always had two pilots on their large planes."

Discomforts ranged from life-threatening to the merely annoying. Have you seen a photo or portrait of a dashing young pilot of World War II, wearing a sporty white scarf around his neck? Fighter pilot Robert Johnson was one of them. He explains that the scarf was not for fashion: "We put a silk scarf around our necks inside the shirt collar to keep from cutting our necks in those wool shirts while constantly turning our heads. That was the purpose of the scarf, not flamboyancy. You had to look backwards 90 percent of the time when you were flying."

Hazards at Every Turn

A pre-dawn takeoff from a fog-covered English airfield could make a pilot sweat in his oxygen mask. Picture in your mind—and hear—"a thousand airplanes trying to line up in groups of 36, spaced two minutes apart, in pitch-black darkness and over an exact spot in the English Channel, at a precise time, make [an] orderly, perfect formation . . . [and] you get the feeling for the high risk of collision," explains pilot Earl Pate. This "demolition derby," as it was known, took place without the advantages of radar. Collisions happened.

"When it did happen, two 65,000-pound, four-engine aircraft, each loaded with bombs and 2,780 gallons of high octane [fuel] made a very untidy mess," Pate says. Then came the enemy. He came in at 300 miles per hour in a power-diving Messerschmitt (Me-109), the showcase aircraft of the Nazis, with guns

Colonel David C. Schilling of the Fifty-Sixth Fighter Group prepares to depart on a mission in full gear. He would be credited with 22.5 victories over the course of the war.

blazing. Many pilots recall the strange shock of realizing, 'This guy is actually trying to kill me.' "

Anti-aircraft Fire

The enemy also came at aircraft from the ground. Many German cities and key industrial sites were protected by numerous anti-aircraft guns. At the sighting of Allied bombers, the guns filled the sky with shells that burst into shards of razor-sharp metal called *flak*. It could turn an armored airplane into a shredded wreck, along with the men inside. Gunner Frank DeCicco witnessed a navigator die instantly when a piece of flak penetrated the cabin and hit him. Flak could blow a hole straight through the aircraft; it often knocked out electrical, oxygen, radio, and navigation systems. It could blow off a wing, sending a plane spiraling to earth.

The anti-aircraft guns that sent up the flak aimed their fire using radar. Radar signals bounce off metal to identify aircraft. So the Air Force used a clever idea borrowed from the RAF: Each bomber released thousands of aluminum foil strips into the air. On the Germans' radar screens, the confusing radar echoes from the foil known as "chaff" or "window", appeared as large numbers of enemy aircraft, flying at all altitudes and in many directions, making aiming of anti-aircraft guns very difficult.

The Mighty Eighth also flew hair-raising missions to knock out anti-aircraft guns on the ground. In these dreaded "flak busting" flights, fighter aircraft flew over the guns to deliberately attract their fire, so their exact positions could be identified. If the pilot survived the first pass, he swung around and would dive bomb the gun installations. If he survived that, he was expected to make a third, low pass to strafe the area with machine-gun fire.

The flyers did not relish being human decoys.

"We were shot at; we were shot at a lot," says Craig Harris, "and flak has two ways of hurting you: You can get hit by a fragment from the initial explosion of the shell . . . also, those fragments that go up have to fall back down, and so you fly through this rain of falling flak. And you can get hurt real bad. . . ."

You could also "get hurt real bad" from one of your own planes. In the black smoke and confusion of battle, in pea-soup fog, and with guns in the

Geography Link   The Other Enemy

"To us the weather was a bigger problem than the Germans."
—*Craig Harris*

Clouds, rain, snow, fog, and wind plagued the Eighth Air Force from their soggy home-away-from-home in the East Anglia region of Great Britain. The poor weather, seemingly ceaseless, presented many challenges: missions canceled or delayed; planes that disappeared; bombers arriving at their target to find themselves unprotected because their fighter escorts got lost; missions aborted because planes couldn't find the target. For much of the year, the climate in England and elsewhere in Western Europe was cold and damp, made worse by strong winds that buffeted aircraft. Weather was indeed a fierce enemy.

The troublemakers behind Western Europe's climate are several huge air masses that swirl in and out of the region, pushing and colliding with each other at various times of the year. A cold Arctic blast sweeps down across the broad lowlands on the Atlantic coast and collides with tropical air that moves up from the region of the Azores islands, in the central Atlantic off Portugal. Siberian and Asian air masses can surge into Western Europe. While the warm waters of the Gulf Stream, traveling from the Gulf of Mexico across the north Atlantic, moderate the climate of Northwestern Europe, they also contribute moisture to storms.

Army weather forecasters, lacking today's weather tracking satellites and computer models, tried to predict the unpredictable. The stakes were high. If a report predicted a tailwind to give planes a gentle push forward, but pilots instead had to fight headwinds, the planes might lack the fuel to reach their target—or to return home.

Question: *How do you think changes in temperature, wind speed, or cloud cover affected the operation of U.S. bombers and fighters over Europe?*

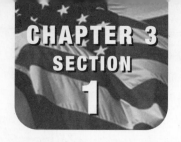

CHAPTER 3 SECTION 1
New Air Strategies

A Turning Point

In the aftermath of Rouen, the Eighth Air Force's first all-American bombing raid, debates of all kinds simmered, both at home and abroad. Rouen had strengthened the determination of General Eaker and the Mighty Eighth. Yet Rouen had not convinced skeptics of the value of daytime bombing. Nor had it turned many heads in Washington, where a critical "guns or butter" battle was going on in autumn, 1942.

How Much Should Americans Sacrifice?

In this case, "guns" were the planned production of aircraft for the war in Europe. The "butter," or basic needs for Americans at home, was of great concern to the War Productions Board, which oversaw the change from a peacetime to wartime economy. The board set goals for production of war goods versus the production of goods that would allow Americans to maintain a certain quality of life.

In the war planning of 1941, the "guns" were winning. The board set high production goals for military goods, including aircraft. In 1942, after Rouen, the War Productions Board declared that the military production goals would place too much hardship on American civilians. At the end of bitter wrangling with the military, in October 1942, the planned outfitting of 215 Air Force groups was cut to 90. The decision came just as Eaker's force was hoping to increase its muscle and win the debate over daytime bombing.

For now, the "butter" had won.

"Pointblank" Policy

In the months following Rouen, the Mighty Eighth took a terrible beating. American losses in air battles were staggering. U.S. fighter planes had neither the range nor the numbers with which to protect the Flying Fortresses. And Nazi warplane production had increased significantly.

At the same time, in Washington, the longstanding argument over the value of strategic bombing finally was being settled in early 1943. Without bombing—*superior* bombing, overcoming the opposition of the Luftwaffe—the Allies saw little chance of invading and freeing France in 1944.

The outcome of this change in thinking emerged on June 10, 1943, as "Pointblank." The order: Destroy Germany's ability to build aircraft. Gain air superiority over Europe. Eaker and his Eighth Air Force sprang into action.

The Eighth had a new weapon in this offensive. In April 1943, a new fighter, the P-47 Thunderbolt, had joined the battlefield. Heavily armored and a fast diver, the Thunderbolt allowed fighter pilots to do battle with the Luftwaffe as never before. Despite American and British attacks on German industry, Germany continued to build more and more aircraft as the German economy geared up for total war. Although Germany was able to respond in the air to Allied attacks well into 1944, the Luftwaffe faced a shortage of trained pilots due to losses.

Germany continued to build more aircraft each year despite strategic bombing attacks. The "Pointblank" policy directed American attacks against this industry.

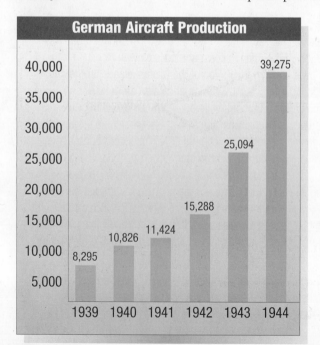

German Aircraft Production

Year	Production
1939	8,295
1940	10,826
1941	11,424
1942	15,288
1943	25,094
1944	39,275

Attacking the War Machine

The bombers approach the target, flanked by U.S. fighter escorts. In the distance, German fighters are massed like a dark cloud of angry hornets, ready to swarm and sting. In deep frustration, the American fighter pilots remain in their escort positions. Under General Eaker's orders, they could not rush forward to try to knock out the enemy and clear the way for the bombers.

So they wait. The two air forces speed toward each other, then collide in a scene of madness. B-17s spin to the ground or explode in mid-air. White, drifting puffs appear against the black smoke; they are the "lucky" crewmen who parachute into the arms of the Germans.

Some bombers reach their target. Too many go down.

Eaker's strategy for using fighter planes was the thinking of a bygone era: Fighter planes escort and defend; they do not take the offensive; their mission is to "bring the bombers back alive." In any case, Commander Eaker firmly believed in the ability of his Flying Fortresses to take care of themselves in battle.

The lack of good defenses took a heavy toll on the Eighth Bomber Command. Yet its men accepted the new mission to wipe out the Luftwaffe and the industries that kept it in the air.

New Bombing Targets

Scattered throughout Germany, factories turned out airplane engines and frames, bombs and guns. They also produced a small but critical component, *ball bearings*. Made of hardened steel, ball bearings roll between two moving parts in a machine to reduce friction. Airplanes could not fly without them.

In fact, the Luftwaffe consumed about 2.4 million ball bearings a month.

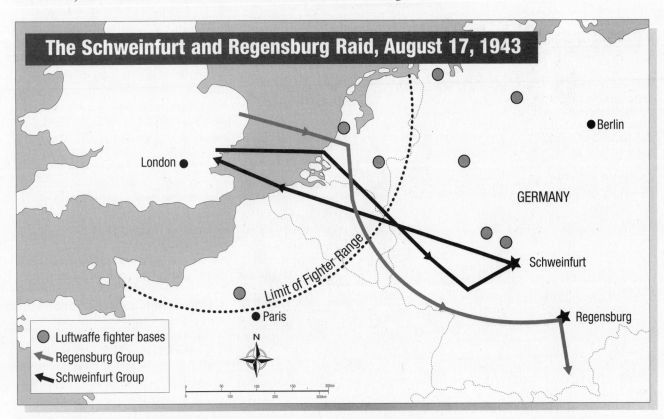

The Schweinfurt and Regensburg Raid, August 17, 1943

Berlin

London

GERMANY

Limit of Fighter Range

Paris

Schweinfurt

Regensburg

N

● Luftwaffe fighter bases
← Regensburg Group
← Schweinfurt Group

0   50   100   150   200mi
0   100   200   300km

One group of bombers targeted Schweinfurt and returned to England, while another attacked Regensburg and continued on to North Africa. Both groups were attacked by fighters from several German bases.

About what fraction of the distance from bases in England to Schweinfurt could fighters travel before they had to return to base?

The Nazis had unwisely concentrated their ball bearing manufacturers in just a few cities, making those locations prime bombing targets. One site alone handled roughly 40 percent of the country's ball bearing production. It was Schweinfurt (literally, "pigs' crossing"), a small and ancient city along a canal in southeastern Germany. Because of the city's immense value, the air over Schweinfurt was fiercely defended.

After spending a year hitting short-range targets in France and just over the border into Germany, General Eaker was ready to put long-distance daytime bombing to the test. He planned a double attack against Schweinfurt and Regensburg, an equally ancient city along the Danube River in southern Germany. The Messerschmitt factory at Regensburg was one of only two factories that produced half of all the Luftwaffe's fighter planes—some 200 planes a month. The Germans would guard it with every plane and pilot it could summon.

"First Schweinfurt"

The day, August 17, 1943, happened to be exactly one year since the bombing of Rouen, a simple mission involving only 12 airplanes. This time, more than 3,300 airmen in 376 planes headed for the two targets. This was the first U.S. mission involving more than 300 aircraft; it was the first to plunge into the distant interior of Germany.

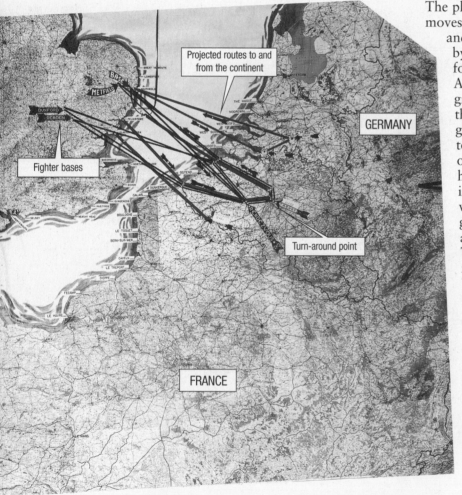

Everyone knew this would be a historic day. The plan of attack was an elaborate set of moves that depended on precise timing and certain expected counter-moves by the Germans. The two attack forces would cross into Germany. Abruptly they would split, one group heading to Schweinfurt and the other to Regensburg. The second group undoubtedly would have to slash through the expected Nazi onslaught to get to Regensburg; however, various diversions, including course heading changes, were supposed to allow the first group to slip Germany's defenses and make the trip to Schweinfurt. The Schweinfurt group would return to England after the mission. The Regensburg group would head south to bases in North Africa, refuel, and return to England days later.

The scheme would work *if* both groups arrived on time; *if* the weather cooperated; *if* the Germans were tricked by the diversions; and *if* the bombers could protect themselves without fighter escorts which had to drop out not far from the German border. Only one of the elements of this risky plan came to pass: The weather over Germany was clear on August 17. Because of this, the Nazis spoiled the clear view of Schweinfurt's factories by sending up a shield of artificial fog over the city.

A map board from an airbase in England indicates the limits of fighter range for one mission in the summer of 1943. Fighters could cross the North Sea and English Channel into the Netherlands, Belgium, or France, but Germany was still out of range.

Projected routes to and from the continent

GERMANY

Fighter bases

Turn-around point

FRANCE

Outcome: Disaster—and Determination

For the Americans, virtually everything that could go wrong did.

"It was just pandemonium."

". . . like wolves on wounded deer."

"Their fire was murderous."

"I had the distinct feeling of being trapped."

"Cannon fire scorched the sky."

"B-17s dropping out in every stage of distress. . . ."

Many veterans have tried to find words to describe the shock and horror of that day. It remains indescribable. Radar alerted the Nazis almost immediately, and hundreds of Luftwaffe fighters raced to defend the German homeland. As soon as the fighter escorts peeled away, the enemy pounced on the first group of 146 unaccompanied B-17s headed for Regensburg. Of these, 24 were lost. The treacherous English fog delayed the group of 230 Flying Fortresses bound for Schweinfurt by several hours. Enemy fighters shot down 36 of the 230, making the day's losses 60 bombers, nearly one in six of those dispatched.

The attack on Regensburg struck a heavy blow on Nazi aircraft manufacturing, although the disruption was only temporary. German ball-bearing production recovered not long after the bombing of Schweinfurt.

Privately, the AAF grieved. Publicly, it marked the day as further proof of the potential for precision daytime bombing.

Opinions varied on that claim. But no one disputed the fact that the men of the Mighty Eighth won the day. Facing what seemed to be absolute destruction, courageous remnants of tattered squadrons battled their way to their targets and then staggered home—only to fight again another day.

"Second Schweinfurt"

The real lesson, that fighter protection for the bombers was necessary for successful bombing of Germany, seemed not to have been learned. It would be learned later, at "Second Schweinfurt", October 14, 1943, when a repeat mission to Schweinfurt had good results, but saw sixty bombers of 320 dispatched lost to enemy action. All but two of those fell to a punishing German fighter assault. Seven more bombers were damaged beyond repair.

These losses, still unacceptable, seemed finally to reinforce both ideas: that of the potential for daytime precision bombing and the necessity of fighter protection for the bombers, as a force of 196 P-47s had insufficient range to accompany the bombers the entire route.

A cloud of smoke rises from the city of Regensburg during an attack.

"Second Schweinfurt" would become known as "Black Thursday." The lessons learned would carry over into the final eighteen months of the war.

A Stronger Air Force

The Mighty Eighth grew in its might as World War II increased in intensity. It had fought its way into existence. As an air force, it had held its ground amid inter-service criticism by political and military leaders in the United States and Great Britain over strategic bombing, over the use of heavy bombers, over daytime bombing, and over precision high-altitude bombing. Eaker's flyers had endured the terrible losses of an air-force-in-the-making at the hands of Luftwaffe fighters and German flak guns. Operating bravely on a trial-and-error basis, they had survived the traumatic years of 1942 and 1943.

Learning tough lessons both in victory and in defeat, the Eighth Air Force at the dawn of 1944 prepared daily missions against the enemy. The Eighth Air Force was provided with a new commander and outfitted with new and more versatile aircraft. In these conditions, the Mighty Eighth carved out a bold, permanent leadership role for American airpower in wartime.

> *"This is a MUST. . . . Destroy the Enemy Air Force wherever you find them, in the air, on the ground, and in the factories."*
>
> —*General Henry H. "Hap" Arnold, Commander of USAAF*

Doolittle Takes Command

When a basketball team struggles for a couple of seasons, management often decides it's time for a new coach—someone to reinvigorate the team and try out new strategies. The stakes for the Eighth were far higher. After two years of high casualties and limited results, in early 1944 the Army Air Forces reassigned General Ira Eaker to be commander of air forces in the Mediterranean. His replacement, General Jimmy Doolittle, took charge of a force consisting of about 185,000 men at 100 bases.

One of General Doolittle's first orders was to change tactics and "free" the fighters. No longer would fighter planes be shackled to the bombers in a defensive position, waiting for the Luftwaffe to attack. Fighter pilots now had instructions to attack the enemy at first sighting. "From now on," Doolittle told a fighter commander, ". . . your mission is to destroy the German Air Force." The order actually came down from General Henry H. "Hap" Arnold, Commander of USAAF in a message that read: "This is a MUST. . . . Destroy the Enemy Air Force wherever you find them, in the air, on the ground, and in the factories."

The order met with enthusiasm from fighter pilots. Bomber crews were concerned that there were not enough fighters to protect them from the Luftwaffe. In reality, however, as new fighters arrived in England from American factories, sufficient aircraft became available for engaging in both offense and defense.

When Doolittle took over the Eighth Air Force, American bombing had not yet slowed German production of either aircraft or ball bearings. In fact, German fighter production was greater than that of the United States.

That fact was about to change.

James Doolittle, then a Lieutenant Colonel, examines one of the bombs his planes would drop on Tokyo shortly before the April 18, 1942 raid. (See page 98).

"Big Week"

The Offensive

Doolittle's staff wasted no time in plotting the destruction of the Luftwaffe. For six days, February 20–25, 1944, the Pointblank targets, Nazi aircraft industries, were to be attacked. But this time they would be bombed repeatedly, whatever the cost. The new strategy added other factories and German airfields to the target list. Nazi warplanes in the air would also be hunted down.

The plan summoned the combined resources of the Eighth Air Force, the Ninth Air Force Fighter Command, the Fifteenth Air Force based in Italy, and the RAF Bomber Command. The operation would later be known as "Big Week."

The new phase of the air war had one supreme goal: to put the Luftwaffe's aircraft factories out of commission. A secondary, but no less important objective, was to destroy the Luftwaffe. This superpower of the skies had to be brought down in order to win the war.

The plan came with risks. General Spaatz feared that Big Week could be a repeat of the first Schweinfurt attack, only on a massive scale. In fact, the plan was approved by Spaatz only on the condition that Day One proved to be successful. If it turned into another disaster, the offensive would be scrapped.

Day One

Big Week, Day One, February 20: The weather over England was overcast with a hint of snow, but Army weather forecasters had predicted a week of clear skies over Germany. From 50 airfields in England, some 880 heavy bombers and 835 fighters lifted off to deliver a message to the Nazis.

The Mighty Eighth showed its muscle, hitting 12 aircraft production sites in central Germany. This time the bombers arrived with plenty of bodyguards, most of them P-47 Thunderbolt fighters. German fighters knew they were outgunned, and were forced to limit their attacks. Only 21 Fortresses and Liberators went down. The attack on so many major sites at once strained the Luftwaffe to its limits.

The longtime goal of bringing American losses to under 10 percent had been met and vastly exceeded. For the airmen who remembered "Second Schweinfurt" or "Black Thursday," October 14, 1943—with its murderous losses of 27 percent—Big Week, Day One, was a day for cautious relief.

The mission continued.

Character Values

Creativity

At the base, Americans applied their creativity to the fronts of their planes. They expressed their originality in the names they chose for their aircraft and in the colorful pictures they painted on the noses of their aircraft to illustrate these names.

By far, most warplanes were named after women: wives, girlfriends, mothers, and movie stars. The most famous U.S. bomber in Europe was piloted by Robert Morgan, who named his Flying Fortress the *Memphis Belle*, after his girlfriend from Memphis, Tennessee. The crew of the *Memphis Belle* was the first to complete the required 25 missions in its European tour of duty and to be returned home. Gil Cohen's plane carried the name *Kayo Katy,* from the boxing term "K.O.," meaning "knockout," and Katy for Cohen's granddaughter. The Eighth had at least three B-17s named Kayo and a couple named Katy. The *Yankee Doodle,* a B-17 with an all-American name, flew the very first mission of the Mighty Eighth in Europe.

Many warplanes bore the names of the pilots' hometowns. One of most unique stories came from Atlantic City, New Jersey, where citizens bought enough war bonds to sponsor the purchase of a P-47 fighter. It became the *Spirit of Atlantic City, N. J.*

The Jackson County Michigan Fighter

A man named Hoffner paints a bomb to record another successfully completed mission of the 379th Bomber Group's Meritable.

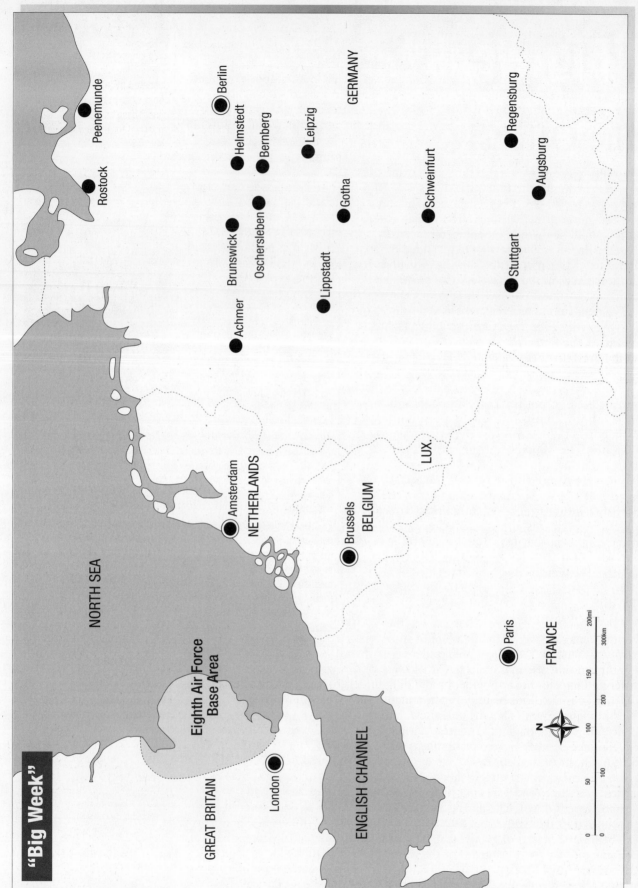

"Big Week"

GREAT BRITAIN

London

NORTH SEA

Eighth Air Force
Base Area

ENGLISH CHANNEL

Paris

FRANCE

NETHERLANDS

Amsterdam

BELGIUM

Brussels

LUX.

GERMANY

Peenemunde

Rostock

Berlin

Helmstedt

Bernberg

Leipzig

Regensburg

Augsburg

Brunswick

Oschersleben

Gotha

Schweinfurt

Lippstadt

Stuttgart

Achmer

N

0   50   100

0   100   200   300km

0   50   100   150   200   200mi

The Eighth Air Force targeted airfields and aircraft manufacturing sites in Germany during "Big Week."

Honoring the American Past

Day Two

More than 700 bombers; only a few lost.

The weather, however, did not cooperate as predicted. Cloud cover over Germany prevented some crews from finding their targets. In England, the expected soupy skies caused terrifying takeoffs. Pilot Ralph Golubock thought for sure his mission would be scrubbed because of the hazardous conditions:

"The lead bomber raced down the runway and took off, and was almost immediately enveloped in clouds and disappeared from sight. We all followed in turn, the planes spaced apart by thirty seconds. When my turn came, I advanced the throttles and immediately went on instruments [using instruments for navigation rather than the human eye]. The co-pilot tried to watch the runway to prevent accidentally drifting off and onto the rain-soaked grass. The engineer stood between the pilot and co-pilot to carefully monitor the engine instruments. He also called out our airspeeds, so I could concentrate on taking a whole lot of airplane off the ground safely. Our takeoff was successful. Upon leaving the ground we were immediately immersed in rain and clouds. . . . The climb was long and grinding, and to our horror, we saw a huge flash of light in the sky. We all knew that two planes had collided and exploded. . . .

"We had to find our proper spot in the formation," Golubock explains.

"The procedure was to fly a racetrack course around a radio signal called a buncher. . . . Each group had their own buncher. Out of all this confusion, we began to form up. First as elements, then as squadrons and groups, finally as wings and divisions. Then the three huge divisions took their correct place in the Eighth Air Force bomber stream."

Closing Out the Week

Day Three: The Eighth Air Force sends out more than 250 bombers. About half of them set out to attack the aircraft factories at Regensburg, where the Germans had not only resumed aircraft production but increased it after the attack of the previous year. This time the Fifteenth Air Force joined in the attack, and the two forces leveled Regensburg. The cost of victory was high: The Eighth lost more than 41 bombers.

Day Four: Weariness sets in. Bleary-eyed pilots climb into the cockpits again, operating on willpower alone. Fortunately for them, bad weather grounds the planes for the day.

Day Five: Every site targeted in the Big Week plan has been hit repeatedly. The Eighth also targets important installations in France. Many sites in Germany took a beating at night from the RAF.

The Outcome

By most accounts, Big Week succeeded in doing significant damage to Germany's aircraft industries. The Eighth Air Force dropped 7,500 tons of bombs in that week alone. The Nazis recovered to a degree, though, by scattering factories far and wide, by building underground, and by setting up decoy sites that looked fully functional and that would lure some Allied bombers away from the real sites.

The greatest damage to the Luftwaffe took place in the air. The pilots of the P-47 Thunderbolt groups got much of the credit, as P-47s made up nearly 80 percent of fighters sortied that week. One fighter group alone knocked out 72 Nazi fighters while losing only two of its own. The Eighth Air Force tallied about 800 enemy planes damaged, lost, or destroyed.

German airplane factories and airplanes could eventually be replaced, but not the veteran flyers whose impressive skills went down in flames along with their aircraft. These veteran warriors were increasingly replaced with pilots with less experience, and the trend continued until the end of the war. This was due largely to the increasing shortages of fuel which greatly curtailed the training of fighter pilots. The Luftwaffe would never be the same again.

Character Values

Honesty

After every mission over enemy territory, the returning crews were debriefed by intelligence officers about what they had seen and done. These sessions were very important for military intelligence and for planners. The crewmen understood that honesty during debriefing interviews was essential for making plans and policies for future missions.

SUNDAY

February 20, 1944
"Big Week" opens with a massive B-17 and B-24 assault on sites including Rostock, Brunswick, Oschersleben, and Bernberg. Leaflets are dropped over cities in western France.

MONDAY

February 21, 1944
617 B-17s target airfields west of Berlin while 244 B-24s attack airfields near Achmer. Bombers are escorted by 69 P-38s, 542 P-47s, and 68 P-51s. Leaflets are dropped over Paris and other cities in northern France.

TUESDAY

February 22, 1944
289 B-17s are sent to attack aircraft factories at Oschersleben, Bernberg, and Regensburg. Bad weather forces one group of B-17s destined for Schweinfurt to turn back over the North Sea and a B-24 group to turn back over Germany and bomb targets in the Netherlands.

WEDNESDAY

February 23, 1944
Bad weather grounds strategic bombing missions. Five B-17s drop leaflets over cities southwest of Paris.

THURSDAY

February 24, 1944
Eighth Air Force bombers attack strategic points in northern France from which Germany launches V-1 flying bombs against Britain.

SATURDAY

February 26, 1944
Final day of "Big Week." B-17s strike aviation targets in Brunswick and nearby targets of opportunity.

Outfoxing the Luftwaffe

Character Values

Self-Control

The ever-present threat of Luftwaffe attacks forced Eighth Air Force bombers to employ the defensive tactic of tight formation flying. Precision bombing required them to fly straight and level during their bomb run—a difficult procedure since it exposed them to enemy flak. Formation flying and target approach required self-control because both were dangerous procedures.

Ever since Pearl Harbor, the giant automobile assembly plants in and around Detroit, Michigan, had been building aircraft instead of cars. The switch was quite a challenge. In the automobile business, manufacturers created one model of a car and did not change the design again until the next year. Not so with airplanes in wartime.

In both formal and informal ways, facts, statistics, complaints, and requests regarding aircraft performance were constantly passed along to engineers at the factories. Mechanical flaws could not wait a year to be fixed. Design alterations, major and minor, went on throughout the war, with the Army pressing for more, better, faster models. A B-17 design might evolve into a B-17G, having gone through at least seven major design changes, like a new model car.

The Research Process

Considerable effort went into determining and taking advantage of weaknesses in German aircraft. Each side competed to out-fly the other. The Nazis had an advantage, because most battles were fought over German soil or German-occupied territory. They could study downed aircraft to identify strengths and weaknesses. If American crew members managed to survive a crash, they quickly tried to destroy their airplane to keep it out of enemy hands, and with good reason. German pilots were known to have flown captured B-17s in formation with USAAF B-17s, but out of gun range. This practice gave German flak-gunners on the ground vital data about the speed and altitude of the formation—how high the planes were flying.

Based on all information, the Army requested changes to improve speed, altitude, flying range, weapons, armor, and payload—the total amount of bombs a plane could carry. Crewmen reported problems from guns that iced up at high altitudes to planes with unsteady or sluggish handling to lack of protection for crew members. Aircraft designers often faced a tradeoff between speed and add-ons, such as more armor and guns. Every additional nut and bolt could make the planes heavier, slowing them down.

A British policeman and soldier investigate a German Heinkel-HE 111 bomber that crashed south of London.

Science Link | Spies in the Skies

After the bombs dropped and the smoke began to clear, a different type of airman went to work. Armed with cameras along with their guns, reconnaissance photographers swept across smoldering bomb sites to capture images of the hits—or misses.

Over Rouen, over Regensburg, over Schweinfurt, their cameras clicked. Flying in special photo reconnaissance aircraft, the men in these special units processed their film in onboard darkrooms to get immediate images. Photo interpreters accompanied the photographers in order to provide instant, expert analysis of the situation on the ground and radio the information back to headquarters.

Intelligence workers prepare for a briefing before a mission.

The "father" of aerial photography was George Goddard, a controversial figure who saw, early on, the necessity of good photo reconnaissance and pressed the Army to pursue it. Along the way, he invented revolutionary photography equipment, including long-range and high-altitude camera lenses and the first night photography equipment. He developed procedures for conducting reconnaissance, and he served in the 325th Photo Reconnaissance Wing of the Eighth Air Force.

Despite Goddard's early warnings, the Army was slow to develop specialized aircraft with the speed, altitude, or distance to fly safely through hazardous sites. Sometimes, P-51 Mustang fighters had to accompany the recon planes for protection. Still, the missions were wracked with hazards.

Aerial photography had a multitude of uses, including mapmaking. Recon for the Mighty Eighth consisted mainly of bomb damage assessments (BDAs), photos of German airfields and of areas with heavy concentrations of flak. This valuable information helped Eighth Air Force planners make quick and better strategy decisions, and it allowed many airmen to avoid areas of heavy flak.

Elaborate briefing models based on reconnaissance photographs helped crews identify targets.

Photo reconnaissance could not solve every problem. If the bombers were on a bomb run to their target, they often had to fly through flak because that was what the mission required.

Question: Why are reconnaissance photographers referred to as the "unrecognized heroes" of World War II?

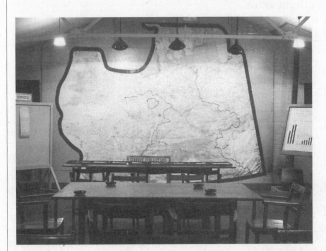

Intelligence reports were used to create maps of the situation on the ground.

In desperation, pilots and mechanics sometimes had to solve problems by themselves at the airfields. One strange but serious problem involved the lack of armor plating under the belly of the aircraft. On a bombing run, flak from below could pierce the skin of the plane, instantly killing many crewmen. According to one story, pilots may even have placed lids taken from mess hall pans under their seats for additional flak protection.

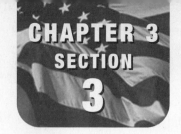

**CHAPTER 3
SECTION
3**

On the Ground

Keeping the Planes Flying

Every bomber or fighter that flew over Europe, and every crewman aboard, stayed aloft and stayed strong because of talented, dedicated service men and women on the ground. From mechanics to medics, support teams worked diligently, often under great physical strain in trying weather conditions, to keep Eighth Air Force operations running smoothly.

By early 1945, the Eighth was able to launch more than 2,000 heavy bombers and over 900 fighters against the Nazis in Europe. Each of those bombers required a seven-member crew on the ground to service it, not counting bomb haulers, refuelers, and ordnance men. Every day ground crews carried the lives of thousands of men in their hands.

Starting from scratch, the ground crews learned a wide spectrum of skills, many of them on the job. Under the pressure of readying the aircraft missions, the AAF's British and American maintenance workers would hone their skills quickly.

Training New Mechanics

During the course of the World War II, aircraft maintenance courses produced some 700,000 graduates. Bob Lyons became one of them. He had joined the service hoping to get into flight school.

"I was too tall at six feet, five inches," said Lyons. "I had always loved to work on cars. They sent me to the Air Force School in Lincoln, Nebraska," and then on to

> *"[The ground crews] had their orders, and worked well into the night, even through it, helping other crews if necessary."*
>
> —Tommy Hayes

Damaged planes like this B-17 had to be quickly repaired and returned to service.

aircraft maintenance schools for the P-51 and the P-47. He arrived in England on July 4, 1943. "The work schedule consisted of inspections—daily preflight [checks], and starting and running the ship[s]." After a mission, "complaints, if any, from the pilots were taken care of." Besides daily inspections, the aircraft got a thorough inspection after every 25 hours in the air, and again at 50 hours and 100 hours.

Ground crews patched up planes damaged by savage flak and enemy guns. They checked instruments to see if readings were correct. They replaced parts, installed fresh oxygen tanks, restocked ammunition and bombs, and refueled the planes.

Bob Lyons became crew chief for pilot Robert Powell. "We had excellent ground crews," Powell recalled. "The maintenance of the aircraft was superb." In 83 missions, only twice did Powell have to abort missions because of mechanical failure, "and one of these was a defective radio."

The Routine

Pilot Tommy Hayes had the distinction of having survived a tour of duty in the Pacific in 1942, before volunteering for transfer to Europe. He described the mechanics' life—a life that might not have put them on the covers of magazines back home, but was nothing less than heroic.

"They generally went to work when we received the mission alert late in the afternoon" for a mission that would begin in the early hours of the next morning, often as early as 3 A.M., Hayes explained. "Usually it called for a maximum effort, and specified an estimated time of takeoff. They [the ground crews] had their orders, and worked well into the night, even through it, helping other crews if necessary."

Dedication to Work

Max J. Woolley, a fighter pilot in the Eighth Air Force: "My ground crew was undoubtedly the best in the group; I'm sure most pilots will say the same." His crew worked unceasingly to keep the planes in the air. "They missed meals, put up with the cold, the fog, lack of parts, no time off, terrible housing, few commendations, continual jawing [complaining] from the ground engineer as well as me to hurry and get the planes ready so that I could take it up and probably bring it back full of holes, [with] a burned-up engine, frayed cables or any number of other problems. The only rewards were burned fingers from a hot engine."

As the crews worked, they worried about the men in the air that day. If the planes did not return on time, "we would check with Operations to see how things were going," said crew chief Lyons.

"[Mechanics] put tape over the gun barrels to keep moisture out," says pilot Hayes, "and if the tapes were gone when we landed, they knew the guns had been fired. You can imagine the sorrow when a crew's plane did not return. The sweating went on, because maybe the pilot returned, but landed at another base. That [information] was probably known within an hour or so."

"They missed meals, put up with the cold, the fog, lack of parts, no time off, terrible housing, few commendations. . ."

—Max J. Woolley

Workers prepared and served meals in the mess hall.

Britain's Queen Elizabeth (center) and Princess Elizabeth (right), now Queen Elizabeth II, meet the ground crew of the 305th Bomber Group's Ole Miss Destry.

Personal Connections

During training in the United States, enlisted (non-officer) air crewmen and ground crew shared the same housing, and formed close friendships. This arrangement made life difficult for ground personnel such as Whit Hill, a sheet metal crew chief:

"[W]hen we entered into actual combat operations and friends turned up wounded, killed, or missing, there was great mourning and a crisis in the morale of the ground crews, . . ." Hill remembered. "As a result, flight and ground crews were moved to separate quarters. After that, the ground and flight crews were only passing friends.

"Those days, after all the aircraft had departed on a mission, there was a quiet pall that hung over the base which lasted until word was out that they were 'coming in.' Those who weren't working grabbed their bicycles and headed for the [control] tower building to watch incoming formations. If they arrived together in a good formation, it was a sign of a successful mission and we were exhilarated. If they straggled in one at a time, indicating a bad mission, anxiety showed on the faces and in the conversations as we watched. It was especially upsetting when an aircraft fired off a 'wounded on board' flare." Plenty of flares lit up the skies as wounded planes arrived, carrying wounded men.

A Crucial Link

Mighty Eighth B-17 co-pilot Craig Harris thinks about the legacy of the tireless ground crews:

"What I am still astonished to learn is how many people on the ground had to do their jobs in very trying conditions. . . . They would work all night in the rain to change an engine. They'd go haul the bombs from the bomb dump in the pouring down rain and load them in our airplanes. . . ."

"I cannot pay enough tribute to those ground people who put us in the air," Harris says. "We wouldn't have been anything without them, and they get very little recognition for what they did without complaint. . . . I don't think we should let anybody forget that."

> *"We wouldn't have been anything without them... I don't think we should let anyone forget that."*
>
> —Craig Harris

Medics to the Rescue

In the night sky over England, bombers and fighters straggle in, many with flares firing—a sign of disaster, of planes with wounded aboard or making an emergency landing. Medical teams, with hearts pounding, rush to meet the inbound aircraft.

Bomber crewmen of the Eighth came back with some of the same injuries any Army soldier might have, such as bullet wounds or bodies torn up by artillery shells. Others had injuries that only a flyer would face: hypoxia from loss of oxygen in flight; frostbitten limbs from the frigid temperatures at high altitudes; burns from onboard fires; broken bones and head injuries from crash landings. Fighter pilots rarely returned to base with serious wounds. Flying alone, they had to abandon their planes if they were too injured to fly, often risking death if bailing out over the sea.

The wounded were received into the arms of dedicated men and women, on call day or night and specially trained to save the lives of airmen—if only to treat them and send them back into the skies.

An Air Force Medical Corps

"When the United States entered World War II, our nation's small aviation force belonged to the US Army and relied on the Army medical system for support," explained Lieutenant General Edgar R. Anderson Jr., who served as Surgeon General of the United States Air Force in the 1990s. "By the end of the war, the Army Air Forces successfully acquired its own medical system, oriented to the special needs of air warfare."

Part of the credit for this change goes to Major General David N. W. Grant, who served as the chief air surgeon during World War II. Grant believed that a separate aviation medical corps was critical to the use of airpower as a separate arm in combat.

The Army created aviation medicine training schools to produce highly skilled flight surgeons, doctors, nurses, researchers, and support personnel. Students took medical, surgical, X-ray, dental, and pharmacy courses, among others. The practice of aviation medicine grew and changed as airmen were subjected to the effects of new aircraft that flew faster, farther, and higher.

Medical units were assigned their own cooks, truck drivers, and clerks. Medical personnel often included people who registered as "conscientious objectors" (COs), those who had strong personal objections to war and refused to take part in the actual fighting.

This crew managed to return to their bomber base with a heavily damaged tail.

Personal Strain

Air combat also took its toll on airmen's mental health. Shock, panic, and mental trauma sometimes set in as flyers faced the multitude of deadly hazards on a mission. The fear of being blown out of the sky gripped even the most experienced men at times. Pilots had to deal with vertigo, usually just after switching from visual contact with the environment to instrument flying. Gunners were vulnerable to flak and gunfire from enemy fighters; they also were threatened by frostbite as only a silk glove protected the hand on the trigger from the cold air. Navigators faced the pressure of guiding the plane in storms and finding the safe way home before the fuel ran out. Bombardiers were under pressure to find the target and hit it with bombs.

A crew acted as a team, and each member was responsible for the lives of the others—a heavy burden. Some men were unable to function; some cracked, especially after watching their comrades die in action or parachute to an unknown fate. Air Force doctors had to learn about and attend to their patients' psychological needs as well as to their injuries.

Science Link A Doctor and a Hero

Sometimes asking the right questions is just as important as finding the answers. Harry George Armstrong had a lot of questions about health and safety dangers faced by military aviators. With the Mighty Eighth, and throughout his life, he contributed greatly to the search for answers to his questions.

Armstrong served in the Marines during World War I and then went home to study medicine. After running his own private practice for a few years, Dr. Armstrong decided to return to the military. He became a first lieutenant in the Army Medical Reserve Corps.

The Army sent Armstrong on the path that was to be his life's mission. He was enrolled at the School of Aviation Medicine in Texas and assigned to the Army's Flight Surgeon Training Program.

In positions as both a flight surgeon and a researcher during the 1930s, Armstrong urged the Army to develop better protective gear for flyers. In 1935, he became the director of a new research lab that was created to study and solve problems such as temperature extremes and lack of oxygen on high-altitude flights.

Armstrong's work, individually and with other scientists, resulted in tremendous breakthroughs. He created items that people take for granted today, such as crash helmets and shoulder safety belts. He helped design the first American centrifuge,

A woman works on baskets for Red Cross medical supplies. The baskets were covered with canvas and painted with the identifying Red Cross emblem.

a machine that can be used to study the effects of gravitational force on humans. These innovations came as a result of Dr. Armstrong's questions and investigations. Armstrong made himself a test subject in dangerous experiments as well.

He continued his diligent work during World War II as the Command Flight Surgeon of the Eighth Air Force. Armstrong's team studied what the RAF and the Luftwaffe had learned about protecting airmen. He co-authored the book *Fit to Fly: A Medical Handbook for Flyers,* which identified causes and treatments for stress-produced mental trauma and digestive problems and for middle-ear damage from rapid air-pressure changes during flights.

While with the Mighty Eighth, Armstrong and other Allied specialists worked together to invent "G" suits, corset-like pieces wrapped around the lower trunks and thighs of fighter pilots that were pressurized to prevent blacking out on a "high-G" turn. They also made design improvements to oxygen supply systems and to equipment that prevents frostbite.

Besides his ongoing research, Armstrong developed new methods for rescue at sea. Altogether, his contributions are believed to be responsible for saving the lives of about 2,000 airmen. For these accomplishments—and many others throughout his lifetime—Harry George Armstrong was inducted into the National Aviation Hall of Fame.

An Airfield in Action

Who helped determine whether a mission could get off the ground safely in fog? Who delivered bombs and butter and mail to the airfields? Who gathered information about the success of a mission? Who was there to comfort the dying men flown back after a mission?

A virtual city of workers—some military and some civilian; some American and some British; men, women, people with disabilities—supported the activities of every U.S. airfield in England. Teams of workers in Army trucks shuttled from kitchens to airplane hangars to warehouses, delivering necessities. Cooks worked around the clock preparing and serving meals—breakfast before sunrise, dinner for war-weary flyers arriving long after sundown. They used supplies that were shipped in, and scoured local English markets and farms for meat and other fresh foods. Thus, Eighth Air Force personnel were the best fed people in England during World War II, while English civilians got by with meager rations even more limited than what American civilians received.

Lines of Communication

By today's standards, communications were primitive. Yet workers answered telephones, received and delivered urgent messages that came over the electronic teletype machines, and communicated by radio with personnel in the skies and on the ground. Information on enemy positions, shifting weather conditions, airplanes in distress, orders to abort missions, and other urgent messages flew back and forth across radio frequencies. Communication was the heartbeat of the air command.

Legions of clerks handled mountains of paperwork in an era without computers, fax machines, copiers, or even an electric typewriter. Women filled many of these jobs, although not on combat airbases in England, because most able men of 18 to 35 years of age were in service. At a bristling pace, on a regulation manual typewriter, women typed up battle reports, lists of the dead and injured and missing, and the horrible letters to parents, beginning with, "We regret to inform you that your son, . . ."

Army chaplains—men of compassion and patience, knowledgeable in the beliefs and customs of many religions—comforted the dying, consoled the grieving, and tended to frightened flyers who had to live through the terror of another mission.

Espionage

Other men and women in the service of the Mighty Eighth performed the dangerous work of spying and reconnaissance, the gathering of information about enemy plans, positions, and strategies. Actor Clark Gable, one of America's heart-throbs, served as a gunner and photographer. He and other reconnaissance specialists flew over potential bombing targets, and sites already bombed, to help planners determine the next moves. (See page 63.)

Espionage worked in both directions. Nearly every base was close to an English village, and the Eighth maintained enhanced security to prevent German agents from taking advantage of civilian access to the base.

The operation of an airfield was truly a miracle of cooperation and dedication to duty. This feat of teamwork supported the Mighty Eighth through victories and defeats; through Rouen and Regensburg and Schweinfurt; and soon, onward to the Nazis' den of operations, Berlin.

Women worked at HQ in England, but not on combat air bases.

Should the United States bomb Auschwitz?

Some decisions can be very difficult to make, particularly in wartime. One way to learn decision-making skills is to look at the choices that national leaders have made and how they made them.

In 1944, the United States faced a difficult choice regarding the concentration camp at Auschwitz. More than 1 million people, primarily Jews, were murdered there by the Nazis. Many people encouraged the United States to bomb the camp. The information below will help you analyze the War Department's decision through a decision-making process.

Nazi persecution of the Jews was no secret during the war, but Jewish communities in Britain and the United States only learned about the cruelty and extent of Nazi killings in 1942. By the summer of 1944, vivid details about gas chambers, starvation, and slave labor at Auschwitz became available to Jewish organizations and western intelligence from sources in Europe.

Auschwitz was located in German-occupied Poland, hundreds of miles from the Allies in the west and the Soviet Army in the east. As German forces retreated, trains continued to roll to Auschwitz from France, the Netherlands, Italy, and Hungary, bringing hundreds of thousands of Jews to their deaths in gas chambers or in slave labor.

Snow-covered personal effects of those deported to the Auschwitz concentration camp litter the train tracks leading to the camp's entrance.

Many Americans felt powerless to save these Jews from certain death. Most of the prisoners at Auschwitz, so far from the front lines, could not be saved by Allied armies. Jews in the United States faced a different problem. They did not want to divert attention away from the shared sacrifice of World War II for a cause that some thought was specific to Jews and not part of the war effort. However, news of the suffering at Auschwitz moved people to action. In July 1944, the Jewish Agency called for the United States to bomb Auschwitz.

American bombers had the technical ability to bomb as far east as Auschwitz by May 1944. In fact, a crucial factory a few miles from the gas chambers was attacked in August by a fleet of 250 bombers and fighters. However, the camp was at the limits of aircraft range from bases in England, far to the east of Berlin.

Bombs would surely kill some of the camp's prisoners. This was accepted because few Jews at Auschwitz could be expected to live much longer anyway, but an attack could save other lives by closing the camp to new trains. After the August bombing raid, survivor Elie Wiesel recalled, "We were no longer afraid of death; at any rate, not of that death; every bomb filled us with joy and gave us new confidence in life."

Bombing Auschwitz was not the only option. Could the Allies bomb the railroad tracks leading to Auschwitz to stop the trains without hurting prisoners? Attacking a narrow target like railroad tracks was unlike bombing a factory or airfield. It required a sustained bombing campaign with higher losses to the Allies.

In August, the War Department replied to the Jewish Agency that American aircraft and pilots were needed for attacks on the German military and German industry and it could not spare any resources for a bombing raid. While attacking Auschwitz might save lives, it would not help the Allies defeat Germany. The reply also mentioned that an Allied attack could lead the Nazis to take further revenge on the Jews.

The War Department had earlier decided that the Army would not be used to rescue victims of Nazi oppression. A memo stated, "We must constantly bear in mind, however, that the most effective relief which can be given victims of enemy persecution is to insure the speedy defeat of the Axis." The United States did not bomb Auschwitz. The camp, and most of its remaining prisoners, were evacuated by the Germans in January 1945.

Making a Decision

Use the following steps below to evaluate the decision not to bomb Auschwitz. As you read each step, think of the important issues raised by the request to bomb Auschwitz.

◆ **Identify the problem and express it clearly.** First, determine whether a decision is needed; then clarify what needs to be decided. What is the issue you want to resolve or the goal you want to achieve? Describe the two opposing viewpoints in this debate in your own words.

◆ **Gather Information.** Find out facts about the issue. Be sure that your sources are reliable. List two facts and one opinion for each side in this debate.

◆ **Identify options.** Be sure to consider all the ways an issue might be handled. Stating the options clearly will help you decide. Describe the options faced by the War Department in the debate over bombing the concentration camp at Auschwitz.

◆ **Predict consequences.** Identify the pros and cons of each choice. List one advantage and one disadvantage of each option.

◆ **Make a decision.** Evaluate your options; choose the one with the most acceptable consequences. Describe the choice made by the War Department and explain why this was considered the best choice for the United States in 1944.

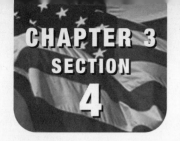
Target: Berlin

Preparing for the "Big B"

He led the first bombing of Japan's capital, Tokyo. He led the first bombing of Italy's capital, Rome. He intended to lead the first bombing of the third Axis capital, Berlin, Germany. But Jimmy Doolittle knew too much. The Mighty Eighth commander had helped create the plan for bringing the Luftwaffe to its knees. And he knew about an invasion soon to come, a great Allied invasion to free Europe and bring Hitler to his knees.

The AAF could not risk having Doolittle fall into the hands of the Nazis. He was forbidden to fly over enemy territory, period.

Doolittle's massive "Big Week" air offensive against Nazi aircraft industries was actually a warmup for the "Big B"—the first daylight bombing of Berlin by American heavy bombers.

A Crucial Target

Berlin—Germany's political capital, a hub of transportation and industry.

Berlin—headquarters of the Nazis' evil regime.

Berlin—home to Adolf Hitler, the man who had plunged Europe into the worst nightmare the world had known.

What airman in the Mighty Eighth did not cherish the opportunity to make that city feel the roar and tremble of American airpower? In the name of all their friends and comrades who gave their lives to battle Hitler's curse, the men of the Mighty Eighth set their sights on Berlin.

Bombardiers, whose job was to deploy bombs successfully, are briefed for an upcoming mission. Why were briefings important?

Ramping Up to Attack

In preparation for the big mission, Allied bombers hit German targets every day in the spring of 1944. Under General Doolittle, U.S. fighter planes made use of their new orders to "attack the enemy on sight." Although Germany did recover much of its ability to build aircraft after Big Week, the Nazis simply could not replace the Luftwaffe leaders and the skilled pilots they were losing. To squeeze the Luftwaffe even further, Mighty Eighth fighter pilots were ordered to dive to low altitudes and strafe German airfields on their way back from escorting bomber formations, and as sweep missions in themselves. Although the tactic produced numerous losses of U.S. fighter pilots, it threw the Luftwaffe into disarray.

Meanwhile, Doolittle had more resources to work with than ever. After struggling for two years to meet the need for warplanes, the U.S. aircraft industry was in full swing, pushing heavy bombers and P-51s through the pipeline. But the number of experienced pilots was not increasing quickly enough to keep up with production. Bomber crews now had to fly 30 missions, rather than 25, in order to complete a tour of duty. Fighter pilot tours were increased from 250 combat hours to 300—about 60 missions. This policy kept the most experienced airmen in the air for a little longer at a crucial time in the war.

Technological improvements strengthened the force as well. New onboard radar equipment allowed crews to bomb through cloud cover. Radar bombing would prove invaluable over Berlin, though accuracy was only modestly improved. In complete cloud coverage, only about 1 in 70 bombs landed within even a half mile of the target. That did not matter, because the target could be bombed more accurately when clear weather returned.

The constant rain of Allied bombs did their work.

Berlin: A Brutal Victory

"**I** hope you have a milk run." A "milk run" meant an easy mission, as uneventful as a delivery from the milkman every Tuesday back home. That is what airmen wished for their departing buddies as they took to the skies, their bomb bays heavy with special deliveries for Germany.

Everyone knew the bombing of Berlin would be no milk run.

Making History

The operation actually consisted of four and a half months of repeated assaults on Berlin, the largest city and capital of Germany. Throughout the winter of 1943–1944, the lighter, long-distance bombers of Britain's Royal Air Force pounded the city at night. America's first strike on Berlin was to be on March 4, 1944. The arrival of the new, long-range P-51 Mustang fighters extended by 50 percent the distance that U.S. heavy bombers could travel with protection, at last bringing Berlin within reach of the Eighth. The vast majority of fighters on Berlin missions were P-47s, although only the P-51s made it as far as the city itself.

"If Berlin could be attacked in daylight, then all of Germany would become accessible to the full weight of American bombs," noted one navigator, Lieutenant Vincent Fox. "For us, the bomber crews who were assigned the mission, Berlin was a giant mental hazard, the toughest of all missions. However, the briefing officer, . . . [a] silver-tongued lawyer from Washington, D.C., had the ability to make it sound like a gallant adventure into the wild blue yonder, to be cherished."

In a way, the officer was right. Historians would later call the bombing of Berlin on March 6, 8, and 9, 1944 one of the top air battles in American history, a turning point in World War II. Yet the victory would come at an awful human cost.

Berlin's historic Brandenburg Gate overlooked a ruined city by the end of the war, after bombing and a fierce land battle for the capital.

Air Force Organization

Headquarters U.S. Army Air Forces (HQ USAAF)

Senior command headquarters for the United States Army Air Forces

Army Air Force

Each Army Air Force was responsible for a specific zone of the war, such as North Africa, Germany, or Alaska. An Air Force included a Bomber Command, a Fighter Command, Ground Air Services, and many supporting units. An Air Force could be a part of the Training Command. The Eighth and Fifteenth Air Forces were under United States Strategic Air Forces in Europe (USSTAF).

Wings and Divisions

The Eighth Air Force was organized into three Air Divisions. Each division, in turn, consisted of Combat Air Wings (CBWs). Each wing was formed from three or more Bombardment Groups and a Fighter Wing.

Group

A combat Group included several combat aircraft and personnel, as well as medical and other support units. In January 1945, the Eighth Air Force included 40 bomber groups and 17 fighter groups.

Squadron

The Squadron was the basic Army Air Force unit. Groups usually were composed of four Squadrons, which made up three combat "boxes" in a Group Formation.

Bombs Away

March 4, 1944. Takeoff time: 0730 hours (7:30 A.M.) Tall layers of dense clouds and snow squalls limited visibility to the length of a football field. Fighter and bomber groups spiraled upward in the dangerous attempt to assemble in formations. The effort fizzled, and soon a recall announcement brought the planes back to base.

In fact, the recall was a fake, broadcast by the Germans.

The hoax worked—almost. One Eighth Air Force group, the Ninety-Fifth, had assembled successfully and decided to proceed, alone, to Berlin. Other group leaders frantically broke radio silence to urge the Ninety-Fifth to return from what would surely be a catastrophic mission. "You'll be sorry!" they warned. With the grim weather and mechanical troubles, only 30 aircraft in the Ninety-Fifth reached the target city and carried out their mission. The wound to Berlin was small but significant. The group received a commendation that declared: "On 4 March 1944, this intrepid [courageous] group led the first daylight bombardment of Berlin by American heavy bombers, a feat for which it has already won world renown."

The Full Attack

Two days later, on March 6, the Americans increased the mission weight: 810 bombers, each with a crew of 9 or 10, plus 800 fighter escorts. The bombing stream stretched far beyond the horizon. A mile wide and a half-mile deep, the stream took more than a half hour to pass over any given point. The force was so extended that German fighters could take advantage of gaps in the huge formation.

"I was the lead airplane on March 6," recalled Bob Johnson of the Fifty-Sixth Fighter Group. "I had only eight airplanes to protect 180 bombers. . . ." The eight U.S. fighters came face-to-face with about 175 enemy aircraft. "We were firing, airplanes were falling out of the sky all over, from bomber gunfire, from their gunfire to our bombers, from them ramming into our bombers. Burning bombers and fighters and parachutes filled the sky. There was no space; they weren't ramming purposely.

"You never saw such a sight in your life," Johnson said. "Bombers falling, parachutes falling, fighters falling. . . . I thought only of survival. . . ." The fighters fanned out to protect the bombers and to do battle with the Luftwaffe. Approaching the city, the bombers pressed on through flak "so thick you could walk on it," as veterans later described, although they had flown through worse flak on earlier missions. Then, bomb bay doors opened, and their payloads rained down on the city.

The Price of Success

Top American generals and policymakers celebrated the achievement in Berlin. The Eighth Air Force had emerged victorious from a major battle with human losses of less than 10 percent. The count, in fact, was a low 6 percent—a figure considered "acceptable" in terms of war strategy. At last, daytime bombing had proven to be effective, accurate, and, in military terms, safe.

The United States and Great Britain issued this statement:

"It is more than a year since [Berliners] were last attacked in daylight, but now they know that they have no safety there by day or night. All Germany learns the same lesson."

A German Perspective

The head of the Luftwaffe himself, Herman Goering, paid the highest compliment to the Mighty Eighth:

"I knew first that the Luftwaffe was losing control of the air when the American long-range fighters were able to escort the bombers as far as Hannover. It was not long before they were getting to Berlin."

Back at the airfields in England, bombers and fighters straggled in—some missing engines, some with sheared-off wings and bellies; some mere skeletons of airplanes. Stunned ground crew wondered how some of the Flying Fortresses still flew at all. Fighters returned with only a few minutes of fuel in their tanks and no ammunition.

The morning light of the next day revealed "a lot of empty parking spaces" amid the airfields, one veteran recalled. Some 69 American bombers —the most ever lost in a single day—and 11 fighters never returned from the mission.

The "acceptable" 6 percent losses over Berlin amounted to 710 pilots, navigators, radio men, and gunners. Survivors grieved, trying to understand why they lived and their friends did not.

Thousands of men became heroes in the skies over Berlin, but few boasted of it. Said one survivor: "If [a man] said he wasn't scared, he wasn't there."

Mission to Berlin, March 6, 1944

504 B-17s and 226 B-24s depart from England, escorted by 86 P-38s, 615 P-47s, and 100 P-51s.

198 B-24s hit the primary target in Berlin.

248 B-17s hit secondary targets in the Berlin area.

226 B-17s hit other targets in Germany.

69 bombers and 11 fighters are lost.

A briefing map on base directs planes to Berlin and Magdeburg —and safely back to the North Sea and base.

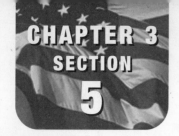

Recognition

Medal of Honor

**United States
World War II
Air Medal**

**Distinguished
Flying Cross**

Brigadier General Frederick W. Castle did not plan to be a hero when he awakened on the morning of December 24, 1944. But at a moment of crisis, he proved he had the stuff of a hero, and his actions would cause him to be awarded the nation's highest military award for heroism, the Medal of Honor. Castle's official citation reads:

"He was air commander and leader of more than 2,000 heavy bombers in a strike against German airfields on 24 December 1944. En route to the target, the failure of one engine forced him to relinquish his place at the head of the formation. In order not to endanger friendly troops on the ground below, he refused to jettison his bombs to gain speed and maneuverability. His lagging, unescorted aircraft became the target of numerous enemy fighters which ripped the left wing with cannon shells, set the oxygen system afire, and wounded two members of the crew. Repeated attacks started fires in two engines, leaving the Flying Fortress in imminent danger of exploding. Realizing the hopelessness of the situation, the bail-out order was given. Without regard for his personal safety, he gallantly remained alone at the controls to afford all other crewmembers an opportunity to escape. Still another attack exploded gasoline tanks in the right wing, and the bomber plunged earthward, carrying General Castle to his death. His intrepidity and willing sacrifice of his life to save members of the crew were in keeping with the highest traditions of the military service."

The Medal of Honor is awarded "For conspicuous gallantry and intrepidity at the risk of life, above and beyond the call of duty." The award is given to members of the military who have served in combat.

By the war's end, airmen of the Mighty Eighth were awarded an astounding number of other medals, including:

March 19, 1943 awards ceremony for the 305th Bomber Group

- 17 Medals of Honor

- 220 Distinguished Service Crosses

- 852 Silver Stars, a military award for gallantry in action

- 7,000 Purple Hearts, the oldest military medal, created by George Washington and awarded to members of military who are killed or wounded in battle

- 46,000 Distinguished Flying Crosses, the first of which was given to Captain Charles A. Lindbergh of the Army Corps Reserve by President Calvin Coolidge for "Lucky Lindy's" solo flight across the Atlantic Ocean in 1927; and now goes to those who perform unexpected feats in dangerous conditions

- 442,000 Air Medals, awarded for single acts of merit, for heroism for every five combat missions flown (later 6), or for meritorious service related to flight, including airborne command and control of combat operations.

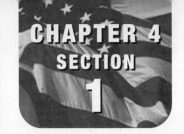

Hitler on the Run

Rising Hopes

The 1944 daily diary of a medical group attached to the 381st Bomb Group of the Eighth Air Force reads as you might expect. It is a grisly, unemotional record of the airmen they patched up, sewed up, and plucked flak out of, day after gruesome day. That's what makes one entry stand out from the rest. The writer departed from the usual depressing listings of casualties to make this observation:

> "27 April—This was the 100th mission for the 381st. It does indeed seem a long cry from the first raid on Antwerp, Belgium, on 22 June 1943. The early raids to France [were] characterized by small B-17 formations and intense hostile fighter attacks and little, if any, fighter support. It certainly seems as though the Eighth Air Force has accomplished a tremendous amount now that it can raid almost any point in Germany . . . without the losses being too severe. The increasing number of crews, friendly fighter support through a mission, and the huge formations that are now being sent over Germany has lessened the mental strain on the combat crew members, and we do not see as many instances of clinically manifested fear as we did formerly. The trend is favorable."

Observing the decline in fear in the men, the doctor draws an accurate picture of the Eighth Air Force at a turning point. Military power was shifting away from the Luftwaffe and in favor of America's heavy bombers, now escorted by fighters everywhere in Germany. The Mighty Eighth was growing in might and effectiveness.

Having established itself as a necessary weapon in modern warmaking, the Eighth Air Force was ready for a new step. It would now prove its worth in working with forces on the ground.

The War on the Ground

From the beginning, leaders of the Army Air Forces sought the ultimate goal of becoming an independent branch of the U.S. military. Army leaders fought to keep the AAF under its wing, but expressed little interest in involving the air force in the Army's ground operations. Air and ground missions—and overall goals—in Europe had been mostly separate for the first part of the war. Each group fought and suffered on its own. Each, through hard lessons, learned how to confront the enemy.

Like the air war in Europe, the ground war was long and painful. It would be two years before the Allies could get a foothold in Nazi-occupied Western Europe. Yet during that time, Hitler showed that he was not the unfailing mastermind he thought himself to be.

Fighters were essential to the protection of bombers and the destruction of Luftwaffe opposition.

Hitler Looks to the East

Adolf Hitler's thirst for conquest had not stopped at the borders of Western Europe. At Hitler's peak in 1942, territory occupied by Germany and Italy stretched across the whole of Europe, from the Arctic to the Mediterranean and from the Atlantic to the Volga River. With the help of Italian forces, the Nazis also advanced across North Africa. Hitler seemed invincible.

Hitler's belief in his own powers of conquest led him to make mistakes. In 1941, he broke a non-aggression treaty and attacked the Soviet Union. Hitler greedily sought the Soviet Union's bountiful resources, including forests, farmland, and oil, to supply his regime. He also looked forward to the prospect of removing the Soviet obstacle to his plans of conquest.

Operation Barbarossa

Hitler sent some 3 million soldiers into this new *blitzkrieg*, opening an eastern battle front to the war. Stalin had recently arrested and executed many of his top rival military leaders in an effort to rid himself of any potential enemies from within. Now Stalin lacked experienced generals to defend against the enemy advancing on Russia's major cities—the capital, Moscow, and the historic port city of Leningrad, known today as St. Petersburg.

At the height of his power, Hitler controlled nearly all of Europe.

The fierce Nazi drive, code-named Operation Barbarossa, sliced through the Soviet defenses at the cost of 2.5 million Russian soldiers. German troops moved deep into Soviet territory as quickly as their tanks could carry them. Soviet troops were encircled by advancing Germans and surrendered by the millions. Others escaped to the east to keep ahead of the Germans. As the Soviets

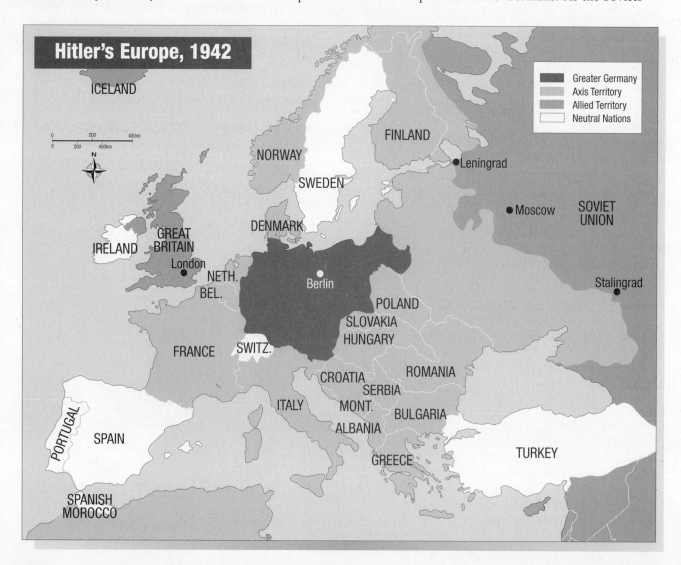

Hitler's Europe, 1942

ICELAND

Greater Germany
Axis Territory
Allied Territory
Neutral Nations

0 200 400mi
0 200 400km
N

FINLAND

NORWAY

Leningrad

SWEDEN

Moscow

SOVIET UNION

GREAT BRITAIN

DENMARK

IRELAND

London

NETH.

Berlin

Stalingrad

BEL.

POLAND

SLOVAKIA

HUNGARY

FRANCE

SWITZ.

CROATIA

ROMANIA

SERBIA

PORTUGAL

ITALY

MONT.

BULGARIA

SPAIN

ALBANIA

GREECE

TURKEY

SPANISH MOROCCO

retreated, they burned and destroyed everything of possible value to the Nazis—factories, farmland, livestock. The Germans arrived at Stalin's doorstep outside Moscow in the autumn of 1941. They also laid siege to Leningrad, waiting for the city to starve and surrender.

The Nazis should have consulted their weather forecasters. The Russian winter arrived on schedule. Temperatures plunged to below zero. Hitler had planned for victory by the end of the year, not a freezing winter in the Russian countryside for his soldiers. Too far from home to retreat, deprived of supplies and warm clothing, thousands of German soldiers froze to death while the Soviets made modest counterattacks. More than a million Russians died in the siege of Leningrad, but they never surrendered to the Germans. By the end of 1941, Hitler had carved out an empire in the east, but he had also won a new enemy and a volatile Eastern Front in the war.

Major Allied Ground Operations, 1942 and 1943

In 1942, the United States, Great Britain, and the Soviet Union met in Casablanca to discuss war strategy. All agreed that they should finish the European war before concentrating their firepower on Japan. They disagreed, however, on how to achieve a European victory. Stalin wanted the others to launch a new invasion in Western Europe to lure the Nazi armies away from the Soviet Union. But the Americans and the British were not ready.

Instead, the Allies attacked the southern side of Hitler's empire. In North Africa, British and American armies fought their way through the desert in 1942. They trapped the Axis armies and forced a Nazi surrender in North Africa in 1943. The American troops were led to victory by General Dwight D. Eisenhower, whose rising career would later cross paths with the Eighth Air Force and would propel him into the Presidency in the 1950s.

North Through Italy

From their secure bases in North Africa, the Allies invaded Mussolini's Italy in mid-1943. Allied amphibious troops, supported by the Twelfth and Fifteenth Air Forces, crossed the Mediterranean to free the island of Sicily, and then moved north to the Italian mainland and the "soft underbelly" of Hitler's Europe. Victory against Italy came within a few months, but Hitler sent German reinforcements to occupy the northern half of the country. The Italian campaign then dragged out for another 18 months as the Allies fought their way north across a range of treacherous, fortified mountains.

On the Eastern Front, a new Nazi offensive against the Russian city of Stalingrad failed, again in the dead of winter. Soviet armies roared back, driving Hitler out. Stalin's forces then began an unstoppable advance on Eastern Europe and Germany.

While Axis armies were being chewed up by the Allies to the south and east, the Eighth Air Force was starting to gain strength against the Luftwaffe. By the late spring of 1944, the tide of the war had begun to turn decisively against the Axis. Victory was distant, but hopes had risen substantially since the dark days of 1942 when the Axis seemed unstoppable.

The Battle of Stalingrad The Nazis' grand plan to conquer the Soviet Union came down to one final, horrific battle. The Battle of Stalingrad, the "City of Stalin," could have unlocked a treasure chest for Hitler. Located along the Volga River near the oil-rich Caucasus region, Stalingrad (now called Volgograd) was the transportation hub for the vast southern region of the Soviet Union. Its conquest would have cleared the path for Nazi conquests in the Middle East and for an assault on Moscow from the east. Instead, Stalingrad became the "graveyard of Hitlerism" in the east, as a popular Russian slogan declared.

The German drive on Stalingrad began in August 1942. First, Luftwaffe forces under Baron Wolfram von Richthofen bombed the city into ruins, killing an estimated 40,000 civilians and clearing the way for German tanks and troops. The Soviet defenders cleverly turned the devastation to their advantage, hiding in the bombed-out buildings and forcing the Nazi infantry to fight an urban, house-by-house battle that the Germans called the "Rat War." Hitler had hoped to take Stalingrad in a few days. The battle dragged on for months, into the deadly Russian winter. In a brilliantly crafted plan, the Soviets launched a counteroffensive that mobilized about 1 million troops, 14,000 heavy guns, 1,000 tanks, and 1,300 aircraft to reach around the enemy forces and encircle them. Hitler ordered his army to fight to the death. Most did. But on February 2, 1943, the remaining men, cold and starving, gave in and raised the white flag. The estimated human cost of the battle: a staggering 800,000 dead among the Axis armies, and more than 1.1 million Soviets.

The D-Day Invasion

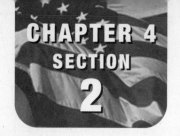

Plans for D-Day

By the late spring of 1944, the Mighty Eighth had become rich in aircraft and men to fly them. However, the Eighth Air Force would soon lose some of its most experienced crewmen, who were nearing the end of their tours of duty in Europe. The losses would deplete the force just as it prepared for the biggest operation of the war: a massive seaside invasion of Nazi-occupied France in June 1944 named Operation Overlord.

After the hard-won successes of Big Week and the bombing of Berlin, bomber crews received notice that they would now have to complete still *more* additional missions—30 instead of 25—to be transferred home or to non-combat duty. Fighter pilot tours were increased from 250 combat hours to 300, about 60-plus missions. These measures provided the Eighth with sufficient manpower for the invasion.

The Union of Air and Ground Forces

An invasion along the coast of France would require the coordination of air, sea, and ground forces on a level never attempted before. The Mighty Eighth was a crucial partner in the greatest invasion enterprise of all time.

General Eisenhower meets with members of the US 101st Airborne Division shortly before D-Day. These "Screaming Eagles" would parachute into France as part of the invasion.

To coordinate the plan, the air forces that would participate in Operation Overlord were placed under the temporary control of the commander of the invasion, Army General Dwight D. Eisenhower. The general's staff proposed that the resources of the Eighth Air Force and Royal Air Force bombers be used to bomb transportation centers in France to prevent German armies from rushing to the invasion site along the French coast.

Eighth Air Force leaders strongly opposed the plan, wanting to continue the Pointblank operation against the Luftwaffe to prevent it from rebuilding. They also believed that bombing the rail yards would not lure the Luftwaffe into the open where it could be attacked.

The Luftwaffe was facing a shortage of pilots because of losses incurred in the Spring of 1944. The Luftwaffe devoted its slim air resources into defending more critical sites, such as oil refineries. AAF leaders favored hitting the refineries. They also supported a plan to bomb major bridges in France to slow down the German advance to the beaches of France. The Ninth Air Force would hit railway and canal transportation behind German lines.

In the end, various air force groups carried out all of these plans with success. As Operation Overlord approached, the Luftwaffe suffered losses of pilots, fuel, and airfields. The stage was now set for D-Day.

Return to the Continent

"Everybody really [started] talking about this invasion that should be coming up soon," said Wil Richardson, a gunner who had arrived in England in April 1944. "All crew members had to carry their sidearms [pistols] . . . at all times on the base. The ground crews were given various kinds of shoulder weapons to carry with them as they worked on the airplanes. We were told to do this because they expected German paratroopers to come in to louse up any invasion plans that were being put together."

Most people in the military did not know when D-Day would occur or where the invasion would take place. The Nazis, from Hitler on down, did not know, either. Good weather would be an essential prerequisite.

The Plan

The operation hinged on keeping the Nazis guessing. The Germans knew that the attack would be an *amphibious* (water) landing of troops and tanks, and that it would occur somewhere along the extensive coastline of Western Europe.

The Germans had done their best to prepare for the expected invasion. They placed 59 army divisions in fixed positions along the Belgian and French coast, along with mobile units that could move quickly to hot spots as they were needed. At the coastline itself, the Nazis under General Erwin Rommel laid down deadly obstacles to the invaders: underwater barricades to wreck ships and minefields to stop troops at the beaches. German gunners holed up in underground bunkers atop cliffs that overlooked much of the beaches. As the Allied armies landed, the Germans, from their high perches, could shoot down at them as they came ashore on the open beaches.

To counter the German threat and make the way safer for the invasion force, Eisenhower ordered the bombing of Nazi-held sites along large stretches of the French coastline. The bombings, in the first few days of June 1944, "softened up" coastal defenses from Calais to Brest and left the Germans uncertain of the landing location.

Allied troops based in Britain invaded Normandy at five beaches: Utah, Omaha, Gold, Juno, and Sword.

The Fleet

General Eisenhower had assembled the largest invasion force in the history of the world. It included more than 7,000 aircraft, 1,200 fighting ships, 4,100 landing craft, 800 transport ships, and hundreds of tanks. More than 132,000 troops would pour out of transport ships and onto the five

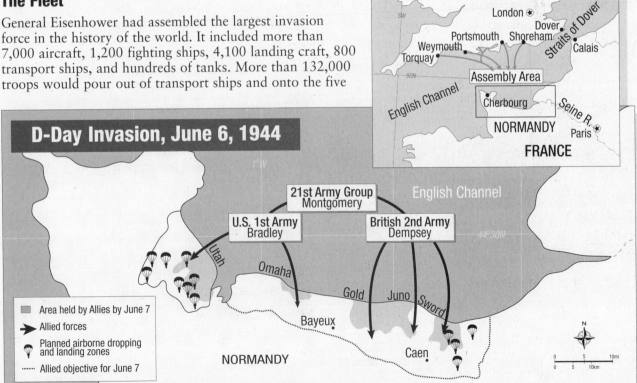

D-Day Invasion, June 6, 1944

21st Army Group
Montgomery

U.S. 1st Army
Bradley

British 2nd Army
Dempsey

English Channel

Utah · Omaha · Gold · Juno · Sword

Bayeux · Caen

NORMANDY

- ■ Area held by Allies by June 7
- ➤ Allied forces
- Planned airborne dropping and landing zones
- ······ Allied objective for June 7

GREAT BRITAIN
London
Dover
Portsmouth · Shoreham
Weymouth
Torquay
Straits of Dover
Calais
Assembly Area
English Channel
Cherbourg
Seine R.
NORMANDY
Paris
FRANCE

A Fighter's Mission. Bill Lyons, a P-51 pilot who flew with the 355th Fighter Group, describes a typical mission over Germany in 1944.

Wakeup. You are awakened at 3–4 A.M. You can hear the bombers on nearby airfields already warming up. You dress, eat breakfast, go to the Briefing Hut. Forty to fifty pilots are there, most in their early twenties.

Today's Mission. Escort bombers to Leipzig. The target: railway yards. Flak expected: heavy. Six hours there and back. Watch out for your gas use-up rate. You draw the route on a clear piece of glassine covering a map of Germany, sewn like a pocket, over the left thigh of your flightsuit.

In the Ready Room, you put on your "G-Suit" (see page 68) and your gloves (3 pair!), sheepskin boots, leather flight jacket, helmet, goggles, escape kit and parachute.

Take Off. A Jeep takes you and six to eight other pilots to your planes. You are a crew of one: pilot, navigator, gunner, all in one. You climb into the tight cockpit. The Crew Chief checks your straps. Your start the engine, check your instruments and flight controls, and taxi out with your Wingman's plane following you out to the to the runway.

Tower flare goes up—you take off two at a time, every ten seconds. In a few minutes, the fifty-plane group is airborne, heading to the English Channel and climbing to catch up with your assigned bomber group at the Dutch coast.

You continuously zig-zag above and to the side of the bombers, to keep pace with the bombers, at your higher speed. Your head is constantly swiveling, left, right, up, around. You look out for your Wingman; he protects your tail and vice-versa.

Bandits! Over Hannover, a call out: "Enemy fighters, one o'clock high!" You see them, about 5 miles away, 75 to 100 little dots-with-wispy-contrails, getting bigger fast. Me-109s! You jettison your two external fuel tanks, switch on guns, go full-throttle climb to attack them before they can reach the bombers.

Chaos! As our Group meets them, planes going every which way! You get a deflection shot on one Me-109 as another almost crashes into you going by. Bullet hits flash on his fuselage and wings. He turns sharply, you try to stay inside his turn, firing bursts ahead of him so he flies into the bullets. He dives. You follow, knowing your Wingman is covering your tail. The Me-109 heads for the deck, corkscrewing down, leveling at treetops.

You get off another burst, closing in firing as he turns right, then flips left, then right again. You get a two-second burst into him, his wingtip hits a tree, he cartwheels and blows up under you. Wingman calls out, "You got him."

Get Back To The Mission. We look around, up—not another plane in sight! You're wringing wet with perspiration. You head toward Leipzig, climbing at high cruise, catch up to the last of the bombers, going into heavy, heavy flak. Can't find our fighter Group, probably all over the sky after the melee.

Heading Home. You fly near the end of the bomber stream—its formations now ragged, some planes damaged—heading back to England. Your Wingman still sticks like glue with your every move. The Zuider Zee, a large bay in the Netherlands, comes up below. Enough fuel for 30 minutes. Throttle back to conserve, letting down. Flak at Ijmuiden! Dive to the deck, go left, right, left, right over the English Channel at full throttle. Out of range now. Nurse fuel across water to England.

England, Home. A great sight. You both land with almost dry tanks. Debriefing by Intelligence officer. Tell the day's action. Eat supper. Write mail. Go to sleep at 8 P.M. You're on tomorrow's mission.

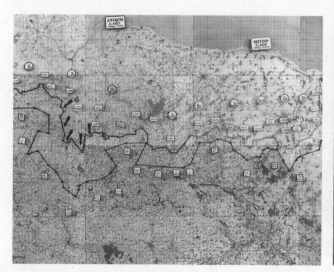

At their bases, Eighth Air Force members tracked the progress of the Allies in France from July 26, 1944 to August 9, 1944.

What do these maps indicate about Allied progress in those two weeks?

Honoring the American Past

beaches that made up the main entry points. They would be joined by another 23,000-plus airborne soldiers who would land near key coastal points.

After landing, the Allied troops would fight their way through the German defenses to capture the beaches and the high ground behind. From there, the massive force of British, Canadian, and American troops would push east and south, freeing the French homeland and on to Germany.

The Battle

Eighth Air Force gunner Wil Richardson and his comrades received a briefing in the first hours of June 6. This was it. This was D-Day. Landing location: five beaches along 50 miles of coastline in the French region of Normandy.

The bombing run had to be completed by 6:30 A.M., to ensure that the landing force would not be bombed as they came ashore.

"We were all told in briefing that the airplanes over the target area would be all Allies, and they didn't expect any German aircraft at all. Flak would be very light," Richardson recalled. His crew lifted off around 3 A.M. and returned to the base over seven hours later. The bombing run came off without a hitch. "The targets' conditions were as we were told. The Germans were not around."

Indeed, on this historic day, the battle-torn Luftwaffe was a no-show. General Eisenhower had guaranteed it that morning in an address to his troops bound for Normandy: "If you see airplanes overhead, they will be ours."

Hitler's Fatal Mistake

Hitler had miscalculated again. Suspecting that Normandy was a diversion for a second, larger attack to the north near Calais, he had held back hundreds of available aircraft. In all of France, the Luftwaffe had just over 300 airplanes to the Allies' 2,500 heavy bombers, 1,500 medium bombers of the tactical air forces and nearly 2,000 fighter planes. The air duel that day was over before it began.

Richardson's crew got a break before being sent back for the second mission of the day. This time they flew in full daylight and through the heavy cloud cover that plagued many of the bomber crews, Richardson looked down. "Hundreds and hundreds of boats still coming across the Channel. . . . I saw the battleship *Texas* firing her big guns across the water to the target areas just beyond the invasion forces."

"I could hardly believe what I saw," said bombardier Carl H. Moore. "Ships of all sizes from huge battleships to fragile landing craft literally blackened the surface of the English Channel . . . you could almost walk from England to France."

A pilot with the 56th Fighter Group snapped a picture of a bombing target in St. Just, France, on August 8, 1944.

View From the Air

Co-pilot Martin Garren's bomber group received a similar assignment. They flew to the now-famous Utah Beach (a code name) to bomb enemy fortifications. Garrin was awestruck:

"I looked to the right and to the left, and out of the high-altitude haze, I suddenly saw what looked like the entire Eighth Air Force, maybe 1,500 planes in a line abreast like the kickoff of a football game. We went on and dropped our bombs. We had expected the Luftwaffe to put up everything they had, because once we got our men ashore—we had 2 million in England waiting to invade— it would all be over. We did not see a single enemy plane or a burst of flak."

"We made two successful operations that day," said John Hibbard, a gunner and assistant radio man. "One to bomb gun installations at Caen [a French city nine miles from the English Channel and a center of German operations], and one to bomb road junctions and railroad bridges. It was a great day. The Luftwaffe didn't dare show itself. We were all out, both the Eighth and Ninth Air Forces, as well as the British RAF. It was a day we will all remember for the rest of our lives."

How should the air force and army carry out joint missions?

Air power undoubtedly played a crucial role in World War II. However, military leaders did not always agree on how best to use aircraft against the enemy. The Army Air Forces favored the strategic bombing strategy independent of army planning. Army officials responded that air support could determine the success of an army battle, as Hitler had proven with his *Blitzkrieg*.

For Americans, the advantages of joint missions in which the army and air force fight together were unproven in 1944. Both Army and AAF leaders were accustomed to going it alone, and sometimes chafed at the necessity of working closely together.

Aerial photo showing extensive ground damage at St. Lô in Normandy.

D-Day marked a new era of unified air/ground operations. The Allies used air divisions to weaken German fortifications before the landing and to destroy vital bridges to slow German reinforcements on their way to the invasion beaches. Once the invasion began, bombers and fighters harassed the German troops with constant attacks from the air. One German general observed: "The feeling of helplessness against enemy aircraft . . . has a paralyzing effect. . . ."

Tactical air support had its drawbacks. A joint mission called Operation Cobra shone a spotlight on the pitfalls. After the initial success at Normandy, General Omar Bradley of the U.S. First Army promoted the idea of using bombers to attack enemy troops and clear the way for an army assault. Operation Cobra called for the air force to support the army even more directly than it had done during the D-Day landing. Neither the army nor the air force had trained for such missions.

Operation Cobra in mid-July 1944 turned into both a triumph and a disaster. Massive bombing of German front lines near St. Lô by the AAF enabled ground troops under General George S. Patton to break through shattered German defenses and head for the heart of France—a major victory.

However, the operation was plagued by problems. On July 24, General Bradley ordered his forces to attack, but then cancelled the mission because of bad weather. Due to poor communications, some of the air crews did not get the message to cancel the mission. They dropped bombs on the target zone, killing some Americans, including Lt. Gen. Leslie J. McNair.

Bradley decided to proceed with the attack on July 25. That day, inexperience with planning joint missions combined with miscommunications between the army and the air force led to the positioning of ground troops too close to the bomb line. Bombers had difficulty seeing and identifying precise targets and Allied soldiers lost their lives. Although the bombers were blameless for the mix-up, the incident interfered with the Allied offensive, lowered morale and raised tensions between army and air force leaders. Despite all these problems, the army was able to break through German lines at St. Lô, thanks in large part to bombardment by the AAF.

The concept of the joint mission was vindicated five months later during the Battle of the Bulge. A German attack on a weakly defended position in the Ardennes forest of Belgium on December 16, 1944, took the Allies by surprise. Hitler chose the date because he knew that bad winter weather would prevent the Allied air forces from supporting their troops on the ground. From December 16 to December 22, General Patton struggled to bring reinforcements to encircled troops. On December 23, the weather finally cleared. Immediately, Allied tactical air forces attacked German lines. Airplanes also dropped vital supplies to struggling army divisions. Together, the army and the air force forced the German army to retreat on December 25. The tide of the battle turned decisively in favor of the Allies. Hitler's last offensive on the Western Front had failed.

> *"The feeling of helplessness against enemy aircraft...has a paralyzing effect."*
>
> —A German general on Allied air power

Making a Decision

Use the following steps below to evaluate the decision to carry out joint missions. As you read each step, think of the important issues raised by the debate over building new aircraft for war.

◆ *Identify the problem and express it clearly.* First, determine whether a decision is needed; then clarify what needs to be decided. What is the issue you want to resolve or the goal you want to achieve? Describe the two opposing viewpoints in this debate in your own words.

◆ *Gather Information.* Find out facts about the issue. Be sure that your sources are reliable. List two facts and one opinion for each side in this debate.

◆ *Identify options.* Be sure to consider all the ways an issue might be handled. Stating the options clearly will help you decide. Describe the options faced by the Army Air Forces in this debate.

◆ *Predict consequences.* Identify the pros and cons of each choice. List one advantage and one disadvantage of each option.

◆ *Make a decision.* Evaluate your options; choose the one with the most acceptable consequences. Describe the choice made by the military in 1944 and explain why this was considered the best choice.

From Normandy to Germany

(See page 84.)

From June into November 1944, Allied ground forces made a stunning and hard-fought 250-mile drive through France to the border of Germany. The drive featured a breakout by U.S. armored forces under General George Patton, who led from the front in his jeep. The right flank of his army was covered solely by Ninth Air Force P-47s during the sweep across France.

Some French forces proudly joined in the liberation of their country, which had suffered so terribly at the hands of the Nazis. On August 25, 1944, Free French forces which had fought in Normandy entered Paris and received the surrender of German forces in the city.

During the post-D-Day campaign to destroy Hitler, new questions arose about the role of the Mighty Eighth and its heavy bombers. (See page 84.) Despite this controversy and other serious difficulties along the way, U.S. forces raced across France more rapidly than expected. In fact, the Americans outdistanced their supply columns. With more fuel, other supplies, and manpower, they could have seized the opportunity to sweep into Berlin. Instead, the Allied drive stalled. This delay gave Hitler a chance to reinforce his defenses.

The delay also opened new opportunities for Stalin. The Nazis were learning to regret the foolish attack that awakened the Soviet bear to their east. By the summer of 1944, the Soviet Union, with a rebuilt Red Army, was slicing through Nazi-held lands in Eastern and Central Europe. Stalin wanted to get his hands on as much territory as possible before a German surrender to build his own postwar European empire. He also sought revenge for German atrocities in the Soviet Union that had caused the deaths of millions. By the end of the year, Hitler's enemies closed in from the east and from the west. Before long, they would destroy German's war machine.

Character Values

Respect for Others

Following the liberation of Paris on August 25, 1944, the 453rd Bomb Group decided they would adopt 350 French orphans. They collected, made, and assembled gifts for these youngsters. Since they could not all go to Paris, they selected a French-speaking crew to fly the Liberty Run with its load of presents and Technical Sergeant Reuben Brockway as Santa Claus. This showed respect for others.

A mission book lists Eighth Air Force targets in Germany four months after D-Day.

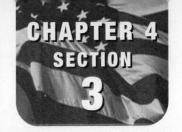

Prisoner of War

One Airman's Story

Luftwaffe leader Herman Goering so adored "knights of the sky" that he supposedly arranged for captured Allied flyers to be kept in better *stalags*, or prison camps, than other prisoners. Try telling that to the men who nearly died of hunger, cold and disease in the brutal conditions.

For 493rd Bomb Group navigator Norman Grant, Sr., it was a short but eventful trip from his home in Minneapolis to a German prison camp. He trained in Texas and he waited for the call to come. Then, with a pilot named George Washington, he and his outfit flew to England.

His first mission was "quite an initiation." Grant flew into combat on June 6, 1944: D-Day.

"Although there was cloud cover over the Channel, we could still see the boats going across," he recalls. "We didn't run into any opposition that day. . . . I think all of us were excited about being in on the big invasion, although we weren't on the ground doing the dirty work."

It wouldn't be long before he found himself on the ground, shot down on his shortest mission, to a German airfield in France.

"My memory of combat missions sort of waned after I was shot down," he says, grimacing a little. "My focus changed from surviving, to surviving and existing as a POW"—a prisoner of war.

A "Milk Run"

What he does remember, quite vividly, is August 18, 1944, the day he flew on what was supposed to be a "milk run" and did not come back for nine months, until after the tanks, troops, and Ninth Air Force P-47s under General George Patton's command rolled over Germany in April 1945.

"About 4:00 in the morning, you got awakened; cleaned yourself up; went down for breakfast. Briefing, 6:00, 7:00," he says, trying to recall the exact time. "Mission on the 18th of August was going to be very much of a milk run. When we went out to our plane, we found out we didn't have our own plane. We had an older plane, an old B-24. And when we checked the equipment on it, I wasn't too happy with the navigation equipment. The radio operator found some things wrong. The flight engineer wasn't too happy. I suppose we could have grounded [the plane]. . . . But the important thing is, as the pilot said, this mission is to obliterate this German fighter base. . . . So, it'll help the ground troops and we'll get another mission closer to going home, and there's very limited flak, and there'd be very limited fighter opposition."

That may have been the way the day was planned; but it turned out quite differently—and tragically.

Although the crew of this B-24 is unlikely to have survived, many airmen escaped from damaged or fiery aircraft and parachuted into German territory.

Under German Fire

"We had very, very heavy and accurate flak," Grant says. "We had no fighter opposition, but flak. The lead plane of our formation . . . was hit and blown in half. And shortly after he was hit, we moved up to another position to fill in the formation. We got hit.

The pilot was killed, and the nose gunner was seriously wounded with that burst of flak.

"The co-pilot called me and said, 'Get me a heading out of here. I think George [the pilot] is dead;' and I said, 'Well, I've got a problem down here with Johnny Doyle, the nose gunner. When I get through with getting him out of the turret and taking care of the problems down here, I'll try to pick you up and give you a heading home.' . . . Johnny got out of the turret and [we] got a 'chute on him and my 'chute on me. . . . He'd been badly hit with a lot of flak, a lot of blood. Then, we got hit again on the other side, and the co-pilot gave the signal to bail out.

Grant's Escape

"I tried to get John around me to get him out of the door, but the front end of a B-24 is rather compact and he just said, 'Go!'. . . So I went out of the nose and assumed that he followed and assumed that, by that time, the other members of the crew had probably bailed out, except of course the co-pilot, who was giving instructions. . . . But, sad to say, none of them survived. I was the lone survivor.

"Something that bothered me all my life, whether something could've been different to get John, the nose gunner, out of the plane, but, although you ask yourself the question a thousand times and the answer is always the same: No, there was nothing you could do. But you still ask the question. So, it's been 57 years of looking for answers and . . . my government told me that all my crew had been killed in the crash.

"The Germans had told me that after I was captured, but I didn't believe them, didn't believe it was possible . . . until I got home in 1945, and my wife told me, yes, it was true, they had all died."

Grant drifts forward in time, telling of efforts to find his crewmen, of a letter he sent to France, and a visit to a village near the site where he was captured. He tells how his crew was buried by the villagers, who treated him royally and gave him scraps of metal that they had saved from his plane. The people put a plaque honoring his crew on their church and built a monument on the site.

More importantly, Grant learned from eyewitnesses that he had not been responsible for the death of his crew's mortally wounded nose gunner, Johnny Doyle. The witnesses told Grant that Doyle was found dead of his wounds, but in his opened parachute some distance from the crashed B-24.

Into Enemy Hands

Then Norman Grant returns to the moment he parachuted out over Nazi-occupied France.

"I don't know how long it took for the 'chute to open. I think I probably popped it as quick as I could when I got out of the plane.

"But you're hanging out there, and you have the strange sensation of going up, rather than coming down; and it's a true sensation, because you have nothing to relate to as you descend. But the picture I have in my mind is looking off toward the airfield and seeing the devastation over there: the fires and the smoke and the bombs that have exploded; and over on the other side, I'm seeing a farmer working his fields, the placid attitude over there, the peace and tranquility, and Hell breaking loose over here.

"[A]s I got close to the ground, I saw all these young German soldiers running toward me, and they were probably a couple hundred yards away. But as

I hit in this field . . . I injured my right knee and my back. And I gathered up my chute. By that time they're not too far from me, and they were, a bunch of Hitler youths . . . youngsters, probably about 14 or 15 years of age. All well armed, but they had some soldiers with them, too.

"So, they captured me, and they put me on the back of a truck. As we passed through a town . . . the French people were standing on the street curbs or their lawns; and they were waving to me and giving the V for victory and the thumbs up, you know. And I thought that was really quite remarkable, because here they were in the hands of the enemy, and they were willing to do that, you know. So, I acknowledged their waving and waved back to them, when I got hit in the head, I think it was with a . . . rifle butt, to let me know I wasn't a visiting dignitary, I was a prisoner of war, and I wasn't there on parade.

"They put me in a solitary cell, and the thing that goes through your mind there is—number one, I'm claustrophobic, and to be put in a narrow cell (probably about four feet wide, probably eight feet long, and not too high a ceiling, and the only opening is a window up near the ceiling, and you can't see out unless you stand on the wooden bed you have there, and then you can see out the window), but things close in on you.

"And you don't know what the present holds or what the future holds for you; so, there's anxiety and—I might as well be honest—there's fear. There's fear of what's going to transpire, of what's going to happen."

The Fate of POWs

Although he may not have realized it, Grant was lucky to have fallen into the hands of German troops and not German civilians. Germany, Britain, and the United States observed the Geneva Conventions, which required humane, if not comfortable, treatment for POWs of member countries. German POWs in American hands enjoyed much better conditions than American POWs in Germany, but both groups were far better off than Soviet and German POWs on the Eastern Front, most of whom died from starvation, disease, and overwork.

Allied fliers who bailed out of their planes over Germany feared capture by German civilians. Ordinary Germans hated the American Air Force for dropping bombs on their homes and would not hesitate to kill a downed American.

A third possibility, if bailing out over an occupied country like France, was to make contact with friendly civilians or members of the resistance. French civilians helped many airmen to escape to the coast of France, where they could try to make contact with the Allies and return to Britain by sea. Others journeyed hundreds of miles south to the Pyrenees mountains and across neutral Spain to reach the British outpost of Gibraltar. Long-distance escapes demanded courage and presence of mind to avoid capture and endure the hardships of travel, particularly for men who were injured in their escape.

Dutch civilians provided one airman with this set of farmer's clothes so he could avoid German capture.

The POW Camps

Grant studied the writing on the wall of his cramped cell. "Some kid incarcerated there had spent time trying to figure out all the capitals of all the states, just to occupy his mind; probably claustrophobic, like I was. And he hadn't completed all of them, so I wracked my brain to try to complete the rest of them."

He saw something else scratched on the wall. "I've seen it many times since. It said, 'I had no shoes and I complained, but then I saw a man who had no feet.' And it helped. Because you were alive. You were alive. . . ."

After being interrogated and processed, the Germans sent Grant and other POWs in France on a long journey to a *stalag* in Germany.

The Fateful "H" For certain airmen, suiting up for a mission over enemy territory presented a unique dilemma. Pilot Ralph Golubock paused as he considered that dilemma. In his hand were his dog tags, imprinted with a simple letter: "H." The letter had deadly consequences for him if he survived a crash and was taken prisoner by the Nazis.

The "H" identified him as a Hebrew, a Jew.

To the military, knowing a man's religion was important, so that if he were killed in action, he could receive a burial appropriate to his religion. But Jewish airmen had to decide whether to risk wearing the "H."

"We knew that Hitler had attempted to rid Germany of all Jews and perpetrated all sorts of atrocities to accomplish this," said Golubock. "Should I wear my dog tags . . . and risk execution if caught? The decision was to be mine alone."

Execution wasn't all he risked. One historian maintains that Jewish American POWs were sent to a special slave labor camp that had the highest fatality rate of any of the *stalags*.

Golubock made his decision about the dogtags: "I put them on." So did another Jew, bombardier Irwin Stovroff. Forced to parachute from his airplane as it exploded over Nazi-occupied Rouen, Stovroff faced his dilemma all over again and made the practical choice.

"I landed right in the front lines," he says. "Germans were coming in all directions. I threw away my dogtags. . . ."

Without his dogtags, Stovroff faced another challenge—proving to his Nazi captors that he was a soldier and not a spy subject to summary execution.

"We moved through the night. And by now the Americans are close enough; so, the heavy artillery shells are going over. You can hear the explosions. . . .

"I didn't have a seat. I was sitting on a box in the aisle. When we got back in the bus, that box had been opened. It had contained hand grenades. They passed the hand grenades out to each of the officers. . . . So I assumed then that we had to be close to the front lines that they would do something like that."

Interrogation

The following morning they stopped in a very small community.

"From there I was transported to a prison in Brussels. It was a pig pen . . . filthy, dirty. And that's the first, what I'd say, thorough interrogation they had. There, again, they told me my crew had perished. . . . They told me the names of the crew. . . . They could have told me what I had for breakfast that day, if they wanted to. They had a dossier [collection of information] on me. . . . They had information on me that I didn't think anybody knew but me. Told me where I'd graduated from school and all those things. And when I had that shocked look, they said, 'Well, you people publish everything in your papers.'

"So they had to have a clipping service that was second to none; and this was before computers. They have all that information on individuals. Quite unusual. Kind of set you to thinking, 'Who's winning the war?'"

At this point Grant's situation turned ugly.

"They threatened me there. They said I'd parachuted into the country to do espionage and sabotage, and things like that. This big German soldier came in, and they talked. Then, he pulled out a gun, and he told me to get up. 'Raus!' He put the gun down my back, and he marched me down the hall. And you think, 'Is this an execution? What's going to happen?'"

The guard walked him down the hall. Then a voice called out behind him. It was the interrogating officer. He called them back.

"It was this intimidation, threat, call it what you will. I assumed it was an execution.

"Then the Hollywood mentality comes in: How are you going to get out of this? What are you going to do? Fight your way out of this. But you're in an institution that's full of the enemy. Why, there isn't much you can do."

Dog tags worn around the neck indicated an airman's name and religion.

To Germany

After the interrogation, the officer told Grant that he would be sent by train the next morning to be transported to an "interrogation center."

The train traveled all day. That night they arrived at a train station in Cologne, Germany. The British RAF, on one of its night-bombing missions, rained bombs all around them.

"They were dropping very big stuff; and that little railway car just sat there and rocked; and you knew that, at any minute, it was going to tip over or be blown to smithereens. Kind of a hard thing thinking your allies are going to be the ones that kill you, but not much you can do about it."

The men survived the bombing, and after repairing some damage to the train the next morning, the train moved on to the city of Frankfurt. There the POWs encountered their first German civilians.

The Germans spat on them.

"It was terrible at the time. But they'd probably just lost their homes, probably lost loved ones, too, to our bombings. . . . We were bombing targets, we weren't bombing civilians. But, afterwards, in retrospect, you think a little bit. I think all of us should do more of that."

Surviving as a POW

During his time as a prisoner, Grant was moved from one *stalag* to another. Had his training back home prepared him for life as a POW?

"For the survival in a POW camp—and there were those that had their mental problems and physical problems—I think you had to face the reality that this was the situation you were in and you wanted to keep yourself physically and mentally alert. We did a lot of walking to keep ourselves physically fit. We tried some athletics, but that was not the place for it; you don't play football in a field full of stumps and things like that."

To keep mentally strong, "you focused on your loved ones back home and looked forward to mail, which is something I never received. The first mail I ever received was at Christmas 1944; and it was a series of, I think, six postcards all telling me the same thing—telling me that I was the father of a baby girl, Carla Karen, and how Momma was doing. . . .

"Margaret wrote letters to me almost every day, but I never received one. She sent packages of food and clothing, which I never received. Here she was taking all this time to do these things, figuring she was helping out, but she supplied some Germans with some more clothes and food. That's the consequences of war."

On the Home Front

Margaret had been pregnant at the same time as Ruth, the wife of Grant's co-pilot. The two women had received notices that their husbands were missing in action.

"You know there were a lot of tears shed at that time. Then, [the women went] to the hospital to have their babies, not knowing whether they're going to have a father. . . ."

After the birth of their babies, Ruth got the notice that her husband was killed in action, and Margaret got word that her husband was a POW. "The whole thing [involves] the family. It's not a *personal* thing, it's a *family* thing. . . ."

"I think of my mother. Four boys in the service, and, fortunately, when she got the report from Margaret that I was missing in action, my older brother was at home on recuperative leave. He'd been shot up pretty bad in Italy. And my brother Dick came out of the tank corps in Italy, and he'd been rather badly burned when his tank got hit. Ralph's aircraft carrier got hit by kamikaze pilots, so he got injured. And what was going on in the mind of that mother?"

Hunger

"We couldn't do much about the food. We lost weight. We *all* lost weight in prison camp. Malnutrition was pretty much prevalent. They brought Red

Prisoners were known informally as "kriegies." This was short for *Kriegsgefangenen*, German for "prisoners of war."

Recreated POW barracks room at The Mighty Eighth Air Force Heritage Museum

Red Cross Recipes. A weekly Red Cross package might contain a can of klim (powdered milk), margarine, sugar, cheese, chocolate, peanut butter, coffee, canned meat, prunes, and cigarettes. The package might have to be shared with three other men, and the German camp authorities often confiscated the meat, coffee, prunes, and other items for German civilians or the camp's mess hall.

The "kriegies" devised ingenious recipes to recreate foods from home using the limited resources of a Red Cross parcel. Combining sixteen slices of black bread, klim, sugar, prunes, and margarine with a little bar of chocolate yielded chocolate pudding. Prisoners topped it off with "whipped cream" made from six heaping tablespoons of klim, nine sugar cubes, and two tablespoons of margarine.

Are there any meals that you could not imagine living without? Find a recipe for one of your favorite meals. Could you prepare it with the items in a Red Cross parcel? What substitutions might you make, and how close do you think the final product would be to the real dish?

Character Values

Patience

Separated from family, friends, and home, patience was an important character trait for members of the military who had a job to complete and years of work before they could return to their loved ones. Prisoners of war may have been in the most challenging position. Their patience enabled them to endure prison and secure a personal victory over their captors by surviving until liberation.

Cross packages, but we got half rations. We had half a pack a week, instead of full packages."

The packages contained cans of margarine, "which was to me as useless as anything," as well as chocolate bars, Spam, crackers, and other basics.

"The Germans supplied us with hot water, and we'd get the powdered milk in the Red Cross parcel, called *klim—milk* spelled backwards—and the instant coffee, so you could make coffee. But the amount you'd put in the cup is what you could get on the *handle* of the spoon, not what you got in the container of the spoon. Everything was rationed. So, you got the taste, but not the full effects of coffee.

"We were on a very limited diet. We got loaves of black bread from the Germans; I think it was made out of sawdust. I know I did the bread slicing, and I think I had as accurate a slice as anybody could probably do; there wasn't any difference in the width of them."

Connections to the Outside

News of the outside world came over ingenious, homemade "razor blade" radios. The building and use of the radios "was a very secretive operation," says Grant. Various people listened to the radio reports and were assigned to stand in a certain place at a certain time of day and pass along the news to a man from each barracks.

"Everything was filtered down. And so that always brings up another question: You tell a story, and it's told this way. By the time it's transferred through four or five people, you wonder if you're getting the same story. I suppose, probably, getting the end result was the important thing, and the fact that we were winning the war, I guess that was the important thing.

"But the ingenuity of American servicemen under adverse conditions is what surprised me. We made our own plates and cooking utensils out of tin cans. I saw them build those little burners. . . . [You could] put a can of water on it and crank away with the little pulleys and fan belts like a forge in a blacksmith shop and heat water and cook things on it.

"The ingenuity of the American serviceman! Under adverse conditions, he comes up with some fantastic things."

Grant suddenly turns grim.

"But to live through it . . . was *more* than challenging. It was fearful. No question about that. But, in retrospect, you look back at it: It was an experience I don't think I would trade for anything. But don't give me a million dollars to go through it again, because I won't.

"I think a lot of us learned something about ourselves that we couldn't have learned any other way. We had the determination, the mental makeup, to come through these adverse conditions. We didn't control coming through it. Somebody else was controlling our lives: the enemy. But, yet, we kept an attitude about ourselves and about our situation that was most beneficial to us.

". . . [W]e came through a period of our lives that most people *never* experience; [they] are never challenged to that degree. So we [can] feel good about ourselves. I think that's important." His voice drops to a whisper. "That I think is *very important*." He smiles a little, still whispering. "Yep."

The Geography of War

In the balmy tropical islands of the Pacific, you shake out your shoes in the morning—unless you don't mind sharing them with slimy creatures that sting. The men learned that soon enough.

For the American servicemen sent to Asia and the Pacific Islands in World War II, daily life presented severe dangers. From the hot jungles to deadly diseases such as malaria, the environment often proved hostile.

The Pacific Islands were half a world away from the British Isles: from the fog-smothered airfields of England, the picturesque farmland of France, and the ball bearing factories of Germany; from teeth-clenching cold and the comfort of warm stoves in the barracks.

In the European and Pacific "theaters," or battle regions, American airmen all fought the same war—a war to crush the dictators who started the war and to ensure the security of our democracy. But they would fight contrasting types of battles, reflecting the remarkable geographic differences of the two hemispheres.

The Empire of Japan

Physical distance made up one of the main differences between the two theaters of war. The Pacific Ocean is about 12,000 miles wide, or about four times the width of the continental United States. An airplane leaving San Francisco, California had to travel over water for 3,587 miles to reach Pearl Harbor, Hawaii. Refueling in the Hawaiian Islands—virtually the only islands in the massive eastern half of the Pacific Ocean—the plane would have to fly another 1,150 lonely miles just to reach the *halfway* point of the ocean, Midway Island.

Midway lay just outside the eastern boundary of a Japanese empire that, at its height, encircled 29 million square miles of ocean and islands. From Japan —an island nation about the size of Georgia and the Carolinas combined— a well armed air force, navy, and army fanned out across China, Southeast Asia, and the Pacific Islands, brushing the northern edge of Australia.

Americans in the Pacific faced challenges very different from those in Europe.

Some of the territories which Japan conquered had names such as *French* Indochina, *American* Samoa, New *Britain*, and the *Dutch* East Indies. Many were directly controlled by Western powers or had strong political and economic connections. These countries and colonies were rich in raw materials that Japan, small and resource-poor, lacked—from rare spices and fine farmland to oil, tin, and rubber.

In this war, an island was not a mere trophy in a collection. If it was big enough to build a runway on, or to house troops, or if it had a bay deep enough to dock a ship in, an island had value. That's why Americans found themselves fighting for a foothold on places that were no more than dots on most maps. Swiftly, methodically, Japan used one island as a staging ground for attacking the next. The Allies would retake almost each one the same way, in a pattern known as "island hopping."

After Pearl Harbor

The sneak bombing of Pearl Harbor by Japan lurched the United States into a Pacific war. In a way, the 1941 attack signaled the style of war to come: an island-hopping war conducted in large part by Navy airplanes piloted by Navy fliers and launched from naval aircraft carriers. In the Pacific, air power was an unquestioned necessity of war from Pearl Harbor onward. The Army Air Forces and Naval Air Forces did not have to prove their value in battle. But they did anyway.

The Western Pacific

Most Americans know about the devastating Japanese attack on Pearl Harbor. Fewer people know of Japan's other surprise attacks that day.

As a part of the Japanese master plan to control East Asia and the Pacific, bombers descended on U.S. airfields on the islands of the Philippines, as well as on several major Allied targets throughout the vast region. The savage attack on the Philippine Islands wiped out roughly half of the U.S. aircraft fleet in the region. A second attack two days later destroyed even more.

Although the timing was a surprise, the attack itself was not. The strategic islands, including Clark Air Force Base at Angeles City, had been poorly protected, lacking radar or even good runways when it rained. As early as 1939, a U.S. military report had concluded that the Philippines could not withstand a Japanese invasion. The report suggested that the territory simply be held for as long as possible. That idea angered the commander in the region, General Douglas MacArthur, head of the U.S. Army Forces in the Far East. The outspoken and influential MacArthur loudly declared that the islands could and should be protected, especially with the help of the new B-17 long-distance bombers. MacArthur did not think the Japanese would be capable of attacking

---

 Art Link **South Pacific**

A romantic American-held island is the setting for one of the most popular musicals ever written: *South Pacific*. Set on a U.S. base and a nearby plantation during World War II, the show weaves together two love stories by the American novelist James A. Michener, a veteran who served in the war against Japan. His *Tales of the South Pacific* won a Pulitzer Prize in 1948.

The musical version of Michener's work, written by the famous team of songwriter Richard Rodgers and lyricist Oscar

Hammerstein II, took Broadway by storm in April 1949. *South Pacific* features a brave Army lieutenant, a local Polynesian girl, a wealthy plantation owner, and a Navy nurse. A dangerous Army operation to capture a nearby Japanese-held island is the backdrop to the love stories.

South Pacific gently addresses the contrast between war and peace and issues of prejudice against the local Pacific Islanders. Today, the show has been staged around the world and in practically every high school and theater in America.

the Philippines before April 1942. He set about upgrading and modernizing the long-neglected airfield. Unfortunately, Japan attacked about four months ahead of his schedule.

Invasion of the Philippines

Situated within striking distance of the territory Japan coveted or had already conquered, the Philippines would add tremendous value to the Japanese Empire. The conquest was swift and painful. No American planes were in the air for protection when the Japanese formations swept in, leveling the facility with ease. The lightning air strikes cleared the way for the Japanese army to invade the Philippine Islands on December 8, 1941.

The ground war to seize the islands and the country's capital, Manila, is remembered for its brutality. American and Filipino forces under the command of General Douglas MacArthur heroically held back the Japanese invaders as long as they could. But as Japan sent in reinforcements, the Allied effort in the Philippines collapsed. General MacArthur was ordered to Australia, where he made the historic and true statement: "I shall return." American and Filipino armies surrendered in May 1942.

Britain, as well, suffered a stunning loss on the same day as Pearl Harbor. Japanese bombers knocked out the British air fleet at Hong Kong, which fell to a ground invasion by December 25.

Japan used its successful formula—air strikes, and then a ground invasion—as its military machine spread south to Malaya and west as far as Burma (today called Myanmar).

Douglar MacArthur arrived in Australia to take command of American forces in the Pacific as Japan conquered the Philippines.

A Defensive War

Despite Japan's rapid aggression, in early 1942, the Allies agreed to make the war in Europe a priority, in order to protect Britain and free the Soviet Union from the Nazi threat. The strategy in the Pacific was different. There, the United States would provide the minimum resources needed to contain the Japanese advances. Liberation was a goal for the future, after the defeat of Germany. At the start, the war in the Pacific would be mainly defensive, not offensive.

But the enemy advance was so swift and strong that it would not be contained. With France and the Netherlands under Nazi occupation and Britain fully engaged in defending its homeland, the United States would have to mobilize to meet the threat in Asia. Given the most slender resources, America's Pacific forces assembled a counterstrike that made use of what airpower they could muster. In February and March 1942, the United States bombed several key islands, and in April, U.S. warplanes dropped bombs on the capital of Japan itself, Tokyo. (See pages 98–99.) The bombings, following months of withdrawal, surrender, and defeat, were a morale builder for all Americans.

Still, by May the Allied presence in the enormous Pacific region amounted to only the continent of Australia and a southern city on the island of New Guinea, Port Moresby. All other key Allied bases in the area had fallen to Japan. Port Moresby would have been a stepping-stone for Japanese control of the Coral Sea region—and for attacking Australia. Japan made its move, sending an attack fleet toward Port Moresby.

Battle of the Coral Sea

The Allies learned in advance of the plan and summoned its tattered Navy. In early May, U.S. and Japanese fleets clashed in the Battle of the Coral Sea.

The battle was a model for warfare in the Pacific, and it contrasted sharply with the style of fighting in Europe. The Battle of the Coral Sea took place entirely in the air. From U.S. Navy aircraft carriers more than 70 miles apart, the two opponents launched aircraft that bombed and strafed each others' forces. The two naval fleets never passed within sight of one another.

In the costly conflict, both sides lost more than half their aircraft. The United States attacked and sunk two Japanese vessels. The U.S. fleet lost three ships before the enemy withdrew. Neither side scored a knockout victory, but the American fleet prevented the Japanese from staking out a new and threatening position in the South Pacific. Australia was safe from invasion—for now.

The Battle of Midway

Still pushing the limits of conquest, Japan then pressed eastward toward its next objective: Midway Island, in the middle of the Pacific Ocean. Besides wanting to capture this island on the path to Hawaii, Japan also planned to draw the Americans into battle to further weaken the U.S. Navy. Like the conflict in the Coral Sea, the Battle of Midway was fought entirely from the air. Navy pilots based on the aircraft carriers *Enterprise, Hornet,* and *Yorktown* fought bravely alongside Marine pilots and members of the Seventh Air Force based on Midway Island.

The Americans managed to catch the Japanese fleet as the Japanese were loading bombs onto their aircraft. The attackers quickly destroyed three Japanese aircraft carriers, as bombs stacked on their decks blew up. A fourth carrier was sunk while it tried to escape. As the carriers sank, they dragged down the 250 aircraft aboard. The victory at the Battle of Midway in June 1942 greatly damaged the Japanese navy and stopped the Japanese mid-Pacific offensive in its tracks.

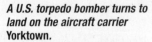

A U.S. torpedo bomber turns to land on the aircraft carrier Yorktown.

Why didn't the Eighth Air Force need aircraft carriers?

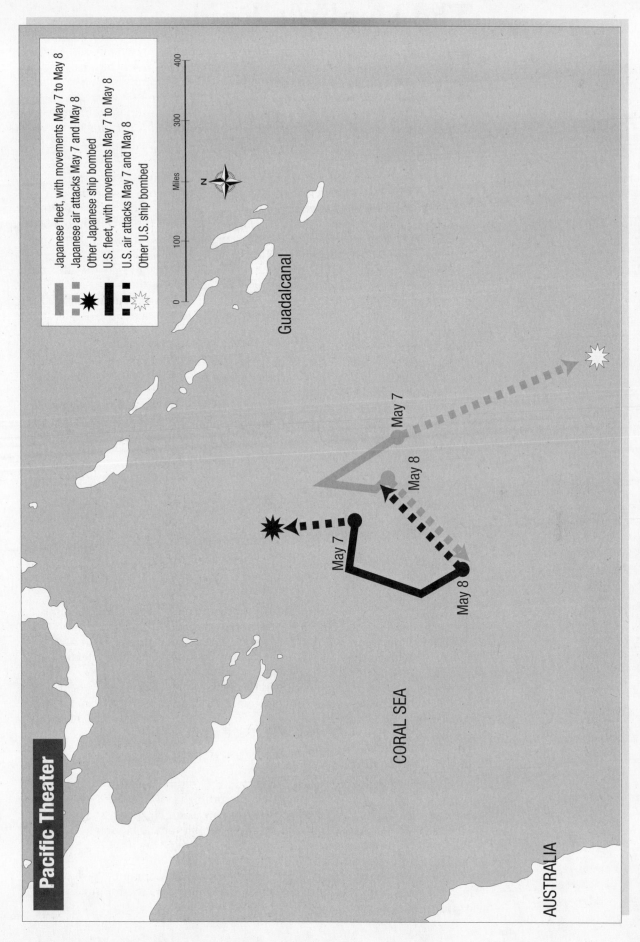

Pacific Theater

Legend:
- Japanese fleet, with movements May 7 to May 8
- Japanese air attacks May 7 and May 8
- Other Japanese ship bombed
- U.S. fleet, with movements May 7 to May 8
- U.S. air attacks May 7 and May 8
- Other U.S. ship bombed

Guadalcanal

CORAL SEA

AUSTRALIA

May 7

May 8

May 7

May 8

Miles
0   100   300   400

N

The most important U.S. and Japanese fleets never crossed paths at the Battle of the Coral Sea, and their planes did not strike each other until May 8.

The Doolittle Raid

Desperate men make desperate plans. Daring men carry them out. Like other Americans, U.S. Navy Captain Francis Low listened in frustration to reports of Japanese conquests throughout Asia and the Pacific Islands. Then Captain Low had an idea.

In ways he could never have envisioned, the chain reaction to his idea changed the direction of events in the Pacific Theater of Operations.

An Impossible Task?

Captain Low got his idea watching aircraft take off and land on the new U.S. aircraft carrier *Hornet*. He had wondered for a long while how America could bring the war to the enemy, attacking Japan at home, bringing off the devastating kind of shock that Pearl Harbor had given the American public. He wondered why a carrier like the *Hornet* couldn't sail within striking distance of Tokyo and send aircraft to attack it.

The short answer: It was impossible. The planes able to take off and land on the small 500-foot-long landing strip on the deck of an aircraft carrier carried only enough tonnage of bombs to cause a minor disruption in the life of Tokyo. The planes that *could* blast Tokyo could not take off from an aircraft carrier; and even those planes could not do much damage to Japan's power to wage war.

But Low wondered if the military had a plane that could take off from that flight deck. Couldn't a squadron of such planes hit targets on the Japanese homeland?

He took his idea up the Navy chain of command. It landed on the desk of a staff officer who was familiar with the planes in the U.S. fleet, having flown many of them. The staff member suggested a medium bomber, the B-25 Mitchell.

The B-25B

The latest version, the B-25B, carried a ton of bombs and could deliver modest damage to long-range targets. This long-range capacity would be important in any plan the men devised, because the aircraft carrier could not risk bringing its aircraft very close to the target cities in Japan. The B-25B traveled up to 300 miles an hour at 15,000 feet of altitude with a 1-ton bomb load.

One problem: The B-25B needed 1,250 feet of runway on a still day to lift its crew and payload into the air.

Could the B-25B be stripped down to the point where it could take off from an aircraft carrier under way into the wind adding at least 40 mph of air speed for the takeoff? One day in January 1942, that's exactly what happened: A slimmed-down B-25B rolled down the runway of the USS *Hornet* and lifted off with 150 feet to spare.

The question that hung darkly in the background of this experiment was, How much fuel could this customized airplane carry? The grim answer: enough fuel to get a fleet from an aircraft carrier to Japanese cities, but not enough to get them back. They could not land on the carrier, anyway.

In the Pilot's Seat

It was James "Jimmy" Doolittle, flying ace and future leader of the Eighth Air Force in Europe, who worked through the problems of modifying these aircraft enough to put a whole squadron onto a carrier. He also assembled the 80 or so men for the mission and led the planning for the bombing run over Tokyo and other Japanese cities.

The plan called for the bombers to release their bombs and then fly through the night to try to reach friendly territory in China, one of Japan's many enemies and an ally of the United States. From there, the crews would be flown back to the U.S. (if they made it to China).

Truly, the mission to bomb Tokyo was a mission of no return.

The men who signed on for the mission knew exactly the chances they were taking. Doolittle would lead them.

Doing the Impossible

On April 2, 1942, the *Hornet* set sail for Japan—or as close to Japan as it dare sail, at least 400 miles from shore. In heavy seas, with a 40 mph gale blowing against its bow, the Hornet headed to the planes' departure point. On April 18, the departure suddenly became hasty. The task force had been spotted by a Japanese fishing vessel. At that moment, Japanese aircraft could be fueling up to meet the American invaders. The aircraft carrier was nearly 650 miles away from the target when Doolittle rolled his airship down the heaving deck, followed by plane after plane. All 16 aircraft took off safely.

They set a course as low as possible over the sea—as low as 200 feet at times—heading for the Japanese mainland. At 11:30 A.M., Doolittle sighted land. He set his course for Tokyo. Nearing Tokyo, he took his plane up to an altitude of 15,000 feet. In five minutes, his crew reached the city, dropped their bombs, and left.

Other Raids

In Tokyo and five other cities across Japan, the 15 other aircraft dropped their payloads and continued on. Eighty men had carried out the plan that originated with Captain Low weeks earlier.

The crews continued on to various destinations in China. Some got lost or could not reach safe territory. Some fell into enemy hands and were executed. One crewman died when he hit the ground after parachuting. In all, 10 men died, 15 were injured.

Even though the Chinese never received notification of the plan and did not provide guiding beacons, Doolittle and his crew managed to bail out and find safety in China. He was pleased to see how many crews had managed to make it back to American hands.

The mission of no return took its place in the history books because it provoked the Japanese navy to seek combat with the United States in the Battle of Midway—a battle that changed the course of the war in the Pacific.

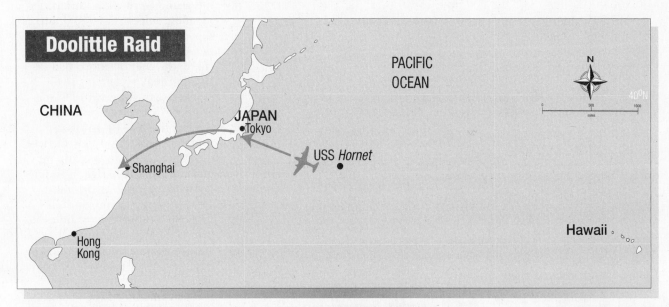

Doolittle's raid carried him far outside the safe range of American forces in April 1942.

Why did the planes have to land in China?

Crushing an Empire

For the eight months or so between the shock of Pearl Harbor and the Battle of Midway, the Allies had waged a war of reaction—responding to Japanese aggression where it occurred—with some success. After Midway, the Allies began a course of *action*, not *reaction*.

U.S. forces would retake the Pacific the same way that Japan had taken it—an island at a time. By capturing strategic islands, the United States would make it impossible for Japan to support bases nearby. Japan would evacuate those other bases and spare the United States from having to liberate every island under Japanese control.

Timeline of Pacific Battles

December 1941 — Japan attacks American bases at Pearl Harbor, Wake Island, Guam, and the Philippines.

May 1942 / June 1942 — American forces on the Philippines island of Corregidor surrender to Japan, joining tens of thousands of American prisoners from the Bataan peninsula on a deadly march to POW camps. The United States Navy prevents an invasion of Australia at the Battle of the Coral Sea.

Japan's offensive comes to an end with a decisive American naval victory at the Battle of Midway.

February 1943 — Japanese troops abandon Guadalcanal. American forces begin an island-hopping campaign toward the Japanese home islands.

Fall 1943 — The United States launches an offensive in the Southwest Pacific.

January 1944 — U.S. infantry land on Marshall Islands after heavy bombardment.

Summer 1944 — An American offensive in the Central Pacific captures the Mariana Islands, Saipan, Tinian and Guam.

October 1944 — The United States Navy destroys the remnants of the Japanese Navy at Leyte Gulf in the Philippines. MacArthur returns to liberate the Philippines.

February 1945 — Marines capture the strategic island of Iwo Jima.

April 1945 — Okinawa, the last island to be taken before an expected invasion of Japan, is assaulted by air and sea. The island falls in June 1945 after heavy casualties on both sides.

August 1945 — B-29s drop atomic bombs on the Japanese cities of Hiroshima and Nagasaki. Japan surrenders unconditionally.

Guadalcanal

The first step was to use naval and air power to gain a foothold at each site from which to deploy ground troops. The island of Guadalcanal was such a foothold for the Solomon Islands. In August 1942, the United States landed 11,000 marines at Guadalcanal, driving 2,200 Japanese into the jungle. While the Navy secured the waters around Guadalcanal, U.S. troops followed the enemy into the tropical wilderness. This was the Americans' first real experience in jungle warfare.

The jungle provided many forms of misery. Moving forward meant hacking away at the thick, vine-covered undergrowth, wading through swamps full of predators and disease, and crossing rivers in full gear. Overhead, camouflaged Japanese snipers in tall palm trees shot at marines as they moved.

After several months of chase, the enemy troops fled Guadalcanal.

So began America's "island hopping" campaign to retake the Pacific. As fast as Japanese soldiers could build new airfields, the Americans captured them, pushing back the edge of the Japanese empire in 1943 and 1944. Navy, Marine, and AAF fliers flew thousands of miles over open water to press their attacks against enemy island bases. Often planes would go out, never to be seen again. Soldiers fought on the ground, sometimes for months, in unthinkable conditions to win back another dot on the battle map.

"I Have Returned"

After the bloody, bitter loss of the Philippines, military planners in mid-1944 did not want U.S. forces to return there. The road to Japan did not lead through the Philippines as far as the military was concerned. General MacArthur complained vigorously, arguing that the United States had a first responsibility to liberate the Filipinos, many of whom fought side by side with American troops during the invasion of the island more than two years before. President Roosevelt agreed.

In mid-October, more than 160,000 American troops invaded the Philippine island of Leyte. After the beach was secured, MacArthur dramatically waded ashore from a landing craft. As the news cameras rolled, MacArthur proclaimed, "People of the Philippines, I have returned."

While American troops fought their way inland, the largest naval battle in world history developed off the coast. More than 280 warships were involved during the three-day Battle of Leyte Gulf. The Japanese high command directed nearly every warship still afloat to attack the American vessels.

This battle saw the first, desperate use of *kamikazes*, or suicide planes. Japanese pilots deliberately crashed their aircraft, loaded with bombs, into their targets. Despite this tactic, the Japanese were badly beaten, and their navy was virtually destroyed.

More than 65,000 Japanese and 15,500 Americans were killed in the six months it took for the Americans to control Leyte. Few enemy soldiers would surrender. The battle for Manila, the capital of the Philippines, took nearly a month. It left the city in ruins and about 100,000 Filipino civilians dead. The United States did not gain full possession of the Philippines until June 1945.

Iwo Jima

By early 1945, the United States had retaken almost all the territory seized by Japan in 1941 and 1942. The closer U.S. forces came to Japan itself, the more fury it unleashed in combat. Two of the bloodiest clashes of the Pacific war occurred within the last few months of the war.

The first took place in mid-February 1945 on a volcanic island the size of a small town: Iwo Jima. Some 25,000 Japanese had dug into the volcanic rock, protected by a maze of stone caves. American bombers blasted the island before an invasion force of about 75,000 marines landed. The enemy proved difficult to force out, and the invasion took a huge toll on both sides.

The Japanese held out for a month. Most of them chose death rather than give up. More than 28,600 Americans—marines, army, and navy—were killed or injured in capturing Iwo Jima. Americans reacted to the victory with both joy and deep grief.

Okinawa

The island of Okinawa, only about 350 miles from Japan, was the scene of another bloody holdout by the enemy. From April to June, 100,000 Japanese made a last stand to prevent the invasion of Japan. American forces put together a massive invasion force, larger than the one at Normandy the year before: some 1,300 warships and more than 180,000 soldiers. The desperate Japanese flew some 2,000 *kamikaze* attacks. Ground troops made suicide *banzai* charges at the Allied soldiers, trying to kill as many of them as possible before being killed themselves. American casualties at the Battle of Okinawa were the highest in the Pacific theater: nearly 50,000. All but 7,400 Japanese and Okinawan conscripts were killed. At last, America had a stepping stone from which to invade Japan.

The two terrible battles showed the Japanese willingness to fight to the death rather than surrender. Meanwhile, in Germany, a Nazi surrender—and a final victory for the Mighty Eighth—was just around the corner.

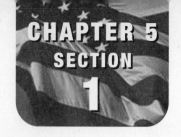

CHAPTER 5 SECTION 1

Victory in Europe

Bringing the War to Germany

The liberation of France provided new bases from which Allied fighters and medium bombers could attack Germany. However, Hitler's forces became concentrated at strategic locations inside Germany, where they could still inflict terrible damage in the spring of 1945. The fight was not over yet.

Yet for America's commander-in-chief, the battle was coming to an end.

President Franklin Delano Roosevelt was losing the personal battle for his health. By 1945, the 63-year-old President was visibly ill. You can see it in the historic photographs of Roosevelt in February of that year, when he met with Winston Churchill and Josef Stalin. The three Allied leaders met at Yalta, a city on the Black Sea, to discuss the future of Germany and of the lands it had subjugated. But one of the three leaders would not live to see the final victory and its aftermath.

President Roosevelt died quietly on April 12, 1945, at Warm Springs, Georgia. Americans, many of whom did not even know of the illness that had stolen Roosevelt's strength, were profoundly shocked. For some, the four-term President was the only one they had ever known. The nation wept.

The man who would see World War II to its conclusion was a World War I veteran and a former senator from Independence, Missouri. Vice President Harry S Truman solemnly took the oath of office of the President of the United States on the day of Roosevelt's death. The down-to-earth Truman would now have the task of ending the war and "bringing the boys back home."

Winston Churchill (left), Franklin Roosevelt (center), and Josef Stalin (right) meet at Yalta in February 1945. Roosevelt was in visibly poor health.

Germany's Last Offensive

As Allied tanks and troops began to move into Germany, the Nazis' defense tightened. In October 1944, Hitler ordered all able-bodied men ages 16 to 60 to join the military in defense of Germany. The combination of new recruits and the return of German forces fleeing from France produced a source of manpower that outpaced the Allies' efforts to boost their numbers on the continent.

On December 14, 1944, Germany rallied for a large offensive, which took the Allies by surprise. In the Battle of the Bulge, so called because of the bulge the Germans created in the front line, Germany spent some of the last remaining energy of its army. Attacking through the Ardennes Forest, the Germans sought to capture the Belgian port of Antwerp. It was a daring gamble that depended on capturing Allied fuel supplies for German use. The courageous fight put up by American ground forces denied Hitler his victory. Clearing weather on December 24 allowed Allied air attacks on German ground forces and turned defeat into rout. P-47s hammered the enemy. The Mighty Eighth dispatched 2,046 heavy bombers against enemy targets, escorted by over 700 P-51s and P-47s. Losses of German manpower and resources in this failed attack prevented Germany from mounting a stronger defense and sped up the Allies' conquest.

A Capital Encircled

In January 1945, Soviet troops advanced to within 40 miles of Berlin. This development forced Hitler to shift some forces from the western front to the eastern front. This helped Allied troops cross the Rhine River into Germany. Ordinary Germans feared the advancing Soviet army above all else. The German army would fight to defend Germans from "Ivan", the name given to the Soviet soldier, even if that left the defense of other cities weakened before the western Allies.

The eastern front had now shrunk to a length of about 200 miles—about the distance from Portland, Oregon, to Seattle, Washington. With every passing day, the Soviet Army controlled more and more of Eastern Europe.

The Role of the Eighth

The Mighty Eighth had two major combat assignments left, and they did not sit comfortably with Commander Doolittle. Churchill wanted American bombers to target the civilian populations of major cities in eastern Germany. He hoped to create a flood of refugees who would clog railroad stations and roads, making it difficult for ground forces to move. Doolittle dissented, arguing that any possible military gain from such a strategy could not justify targeting civilians. The missions went on as planned.

The first main target: Berlin. Unlike the initial bombing of the German capital, the bombing runs on February 3, 1945, were not aimed at the city's rail yards and industries. This time, the Eighth Air Force sent almost 1,000 heavy bombers to the heavily populated center of the city, which housed the heart of the German military establishment: the Air Ministry, the War Office, and important buildings nearby. Each bomb group in the Eighth formations was assigned a specific building as a target. Great precision and accuracy placed 1.25 tons of bombs on each acre of the target area. All 23 Allied bombers shot down over Berlin were hit by flak from the ground. Protecting the bombers were 525 P-51s which claimed 29 German fighters destroyed. German press and radio said there were 20,000 to 25,000 civilian casualties. About 120,000 people lost their homes and became refugees. Thus Churchill's purposes were fulfilled.

The next big target was a city dating back to the 1200s and known for its magnificent architecture and art, a city often called one of the most beautiful in the world: Dresden. But Dresden had military targets, not previously attacked, including a large rail yard, a defense communications center, and weapons industries employing 50,000 people. AAF leaders said the purpose of the bombings was to cut Nazi communications lines to help the Soviets' armies

 Science Link | **Jet!**

In mid-summer 1944, with Pacific forces winning back island after island and Allied forces liberating France, a strange aircraft began to appear in the skies. The guys in the Mighty Eighth had heard the rumors: Germany had invented an airplane with no propellers. Suddenly here it was, streaking by them with a loud roaring sound, leaving Allied pilots impressed—and nervous.

German engineers had developed the jet airplane.

Zooming through the battle skies at 500 miles per hour, Germany's jet-powered Messerschmitt-262 (Me-262) had the potential to extend the European war or even reverse its course.

Jet engines produce thrust for propulsion by blowing hot gases from the combustion (burning) of fuel through a nozzle at the rear of the engine. A turbine—a set of rotating blades like a fan—compresses air for this combustion as it comes into the front of the engine. The compressor turbine is on the same shaft with another turbine driven by the combusting fuel-air mixture. The resulting thrust from the exhaust nozzle drives an aircraft forward.

Hitler now had a weapon that could have turned the air war on its head. But instead he held up the production of jets by ordering configuration of the Me-262 as a fighter-bomber. That delayed production of the Me-262 as an interceptor fighter until the Nazis were suffering a critical shortage of trained pilots and of aircraft fuel. Thus, jet aircraft failed to have a major influence on the war, although they could have made things very difficult for the Mighty Eighth.

When the guns finally fell silent over Europe, Allied troops stood at the end of their long offensive in two lines dividing Europe north-to-south. These lines were determined both by agreements at Yalta and by the progress of individual armies. Small pockets of German troops remained in between the Soviets and the Western Allies, awaiting surrender.

In the following months, Allied troops pulled back to their occupation zones as determined by civilian leaders. Cities liberated by Americans in 1945, including Erfurt in Germany and Pilsen in Czechoslovakia, fell in the Soviet zones of occupation and would fall under Communist rule. Austria and Germany were divided up among Britain, France, the United States, and the Soviet Union.

The rough lines staked out by the armies in May 1945 would transform into an Iron Curtain dividing the democratic countries of Western Europe from communist Soviet puppet states in Eastern Europe. The four powers eventually released Austria as a neutral democratic state. There would be no cooperation over Germany, where the French, British, and American zones merged to form West Germany in 1949, and the Soviet zone became communist East Germany six years later.

Germany, May 1945

Germany, May 1955

Democracies
Communist Satellites
— Iron Curtain

to advance in eastern Germany. On the night of February 13, the RAF hit Dresden with 2,700 tons of bombs, of which half were incendiary. That mix of bombs, because of unusual winter weather, triggered a firestorm that shot fire and smoke 15,000 feet into the sky and consumed everything in its path. Over the next two days, B-17s dropped another 1,200 tons of bombs on the rail yards. An estimated 30,000 people in Dresden died in these missions with limited benefits for the Soviet advance. The city of culture became a city of ashes. Dresden would join London, Coventry, Warsaw, Rotterdam, and Leningrad, all victims of mass bombing, as symbols of the destruction of war.

The Luftwaffe

With the major military targets obliterated, the Mighty Eighth received orders for a campaign to hit railroad stations and small industries in hundreds of German towns and villages. The message: We won, you lost. On February 22, thousands of Allied bombers and fighters fanned out across Germany. General Eaker objected, and this operation was halted after one more day of missions.

Air support was brought in when several Allied armies crossed the geographic barrier of the Rhine River in March and headed toward Berlin. In his combat diary, Staff Sergeant William J. Mulholland, a gunner, recorded the devastation that the Eighth Air Force brought, even at this late stage of the war:

> "MARCH 14, 1945 Now this was my last mission for the completion of my tour. [W]e bombed marshalling [railroad] yards in Germany. . . . The target was visible and we hit the station smack in the center. . . . In all my flying I have never seen so many towns afire and bridges blown up. One city near the Rhine River was getting shelled; we could see the explosions every so often. Another town, very small, was practically wiped out by the bombs from medium bombers."

At this point, most Germans longed for only one outcome: to be conquered by American and British troops, and not by the dreaded Soviets.

The Eighth Air Force, lacking major strategic targets, did smaller chores such as bombing rail yards and oil depots in north-central Germany. Remarkably, though on its deathbed in April, the Luftwaffe brought out one final, frightening weapon: the jet airplane. Bombers from the Eighth and fighter-bombers from the Eighth and Ninth targeted airfields and knocked out many remaining German planes on the ground.

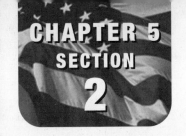

Spring 1945

Hitler's Final Days

As Allied troops drove toward Berlin, Hitler issued a last order that clearly revealed the mind of a delusional madman. Retreating German soldiers should destroy everything of potential value to the Allies: "all industrial plants, all the main electricity works, waterworks, gas works" and "all food and clothing stores" without regard "for our own population." The purpose was to create "a desert" in the Allies' path, much as the Russians had done to the Germans, with success, in 1941.

This order was too much even for the evil men with whom Hitler had surrounded himself. The military largely ignored the order. Holed up in his isolated bunker in Berlin, Hitler made no attempts to flee, but waited, despondent, as Soviet troops encircled Berlin on April 25. The Americans and British could have reached Hitler sooner, but at General Eisenhower's order they held up at the Elbe River so the Soviets could take the city. Under the terms of the Yalta agreement, the Soviet Union would occupy Berlin anyway. With predictions that the conquest of Berlin could cost 100,000 American lives, Eisenhower was content to let the eager Soviets complete the task.

On April 30, Adolf Hitler committed suicide. Hitler's hand-picked successor, Karl Doenitz, took control of the government on May 2, but only for a few days. He promptly arranged for an unconditional surrender and hurried to get German refugees and soldiers into the hands of the Americans and the British.

Last Flights for the Luftwaffe

Hitler's once-proud Luftwaffe also sought to avoid capture by the Soviet army. Jet pilots destroyed their aircraft to keep them out of Allied hands.

Navigator John A. Thurmond of the Mighty Eighth had just been freed from a prisoner-of-war camp and transported to a military base with other POWs when the individual surrenders began among Luftwaffe pilots. "German pilots were flying in from the east," Thurmond remembers. "They didn't want the Russians to capture them. They knew the war was over . . . so, they flew their planes into that base and landed and surrendered to the Americans. Well, there actually wasn't anybody there but American prisoners, so they were surrendering to us.

"One pilot came in a little observation plane of some kind, like a Piper Cub that we had then," Thurmond recalls. "And he got out of the plane, and he took his screwdriver out, and he took the cover off of—I think it was supposed to be a radio compartment, behind the cockpit—and he got this girl out of there. She was all curled up in the radio compartment, and he had brought her in. I don't know if it was his girlfriend, or wife, or what it was; but he had brought her in from the east to keep her away from the Soviets."

Herman Goering, the head of the Luftwaffe and the man behind the bombing of Britain and countless atrocities, met his fate on May 9, when he was captured by American troops. At the famous war tribunal

Character Values

Generosity
The Eighth Air Force participated in Allied food drops over the Nazi-occupied Netherlands during the first week of May 1945. Reflecting a spirit of generosity, these rations were taken from the food supply of the United States Armed Forces without any guarantee that they would be replaced.

> *"They knew the war was over...
> so they flew their planes into that base and landed and surrendered to the Americans."*
>
> —*Navigator John A. Thurmond*

Dutch youngsters beat empty cookie containers left over from gifts provided by Allied forces.

at Nuremberg, Germany, in 1946, Goering was convicted for his war crimes and sentenced to die. Just two hours before his execution, he committed suicide by swallowing a capsule of the deadly poison cyanide, which he had smuggled into the prison.

Operation Chowhound

A weapons plant in Czechoslovakia became the last industrial target of the Mighty Eighth on April 25. After that, further bombing would have threatened friendly forces on the ground, as well as refugees and people freed from concentration camps and POW camps. The Army Air Forces in Europe took on humanitarian missions, to the delight of airmen. Throughout Europe they ferried airmen, including liberated POWs, back to their bases in England.

In a campaign called Operation Chowhound, planes dropped food and medical supplies to needy war survivors. The people of the Netherlands, trapped under German control until the last days of the war, were some of the beneficiaries. The Nazis had cut off food supplies to the Netherlands in the winter of 1944–1945, and Dutch civilians were dying of starvation.

"They placed plywood doors inside the bomb bay, rigged to the bomb-release shackles," said navigator Bill Varnadoe. "The bomb bays were then loaded with food packages. We flew in, very low, over an airfield marked with white crosses, and dropped the food. Our drop point was . . . the main airfield for Amsterdam [the largest city]. Many Hollanders were out waving at us, and we wagged our wings at them."

Victory in Europe

Victory in Europe, known as V-E Day, arrived at midnight on May 8, 1945, when representatives of the fallen Nazi government signed an unconditional surrender at General Eisenhower's headquarters in Reims, France.

John Thurmond was still in a POW camp on V-E Day. He recalls it vividly: "Bullets start flying over us, singing over our head. So, everybody got excited and scared and nervous and happy. . . . We could hear the battle and the artillery going overhead. And about 12:30 that day, we heard a lot of yelling and screaming and cheering. We looked out, and the German flag that was flying . . . was coming down. And the American flag went up.

"So, we knew, then, that we were free," Thurmond says. "I think everybody cried a little bit. I don't think there was a dry eye in the camp. . . . And the American troops came in, actually came into the camp and moved around through us. And that afternoon, probably around 3:00, General [George S.] Patton came in, with his Jeep shined up and his ivory handled revolvers and his shiny helmet; and came right into camp and walked among us."

After months of ill treatment, navigator Norman Grant had been forced to march across Germany in the final weeks of the war. He arrived at a new stalag on April 27, 1945 with a badly infected leg. Only the arrival of General Patton's troops two days later saved him from amputation and possible death.

The Allied rescuers put a disinfectant in the wound and whisked Grant away to a mobile front-line hospital. "They gave me a shot of that new medication, called *penicillin*—just coming into being. . . . [I]t didn't take long at all, maybe a couple of days, and I was ambulatory. . . ."

After being transferred to a French hospital, where he was well treated, Grant and some other men checked in with authorities in Paris and managed to get a place on a "liberty tub"—a ship that brought the veterans home. They were the first POWs to return.

Still aboard ship, the men were asked if they would like to remain anchored in Boston Harbor. "Well, you know what our response was: 'The heck with the celebration! Get us off this tub and get us on land!'"

American POWs celebrate their freedom from German captivity.

Homecoming

John Thurmond boarded a liberty ship that arrived in New York Harbor, the place that has welcomed so many wanderers to America's shores.

"Oh, that was wonderful. That Statue of Liberty, the most beautiful sight I'd ever seen. Everybody cheered, and everybody cried a little, I guess. It was a wonderful feeling," Thurmond remembered.

When Norman Grant's ship arrived in Boston, he boarded a train to go home to his wife, Margaret, in Minneapolis, Minnesota. Grant took a streetcar to the southeast part of the city.

"Margaret was living with her mother and her sisters and the baby. . . . I came walking down the street, and one of my sisters-in-law—she was probably about twelve years old at the time—came out the door, started walking down the street, and she saw me, and she let [out] a yell. She started

V-E Day headlines

running toward me. She stopped, started running back. Stopped, started running toward me. She didn't know which way to [go]!

"Margaret had our little girl with her. If that could have been captured on film, instead of just memories, it'd be a treasure. But it's a treasure just the way it *is*.

"I can see that so vividly." Grant's voice cracks. He says, softly, "One of the greatest days of my life."

For many men in the Eighth, returning home meant going back to the simplest pleasures that had been denied them during the war: "I couldn't wait to get an ice cream or an ice cream soda and a hamburger; because we had had no ice cream; no milk," says gunner John C. Veenschoten. "Eggs and all that sort of thing: it was all powdered. . . . We didn't take sandwiches or anything like that on the aircraft. You just didn't eat."

V-E Day arrived less than a month after the death of President Roosevelt. Milton Lipson was a Secret Service agent assigned to protect Roosevelt, and then Truman, at various times during the war. At the 50th anniversary of V-E day, in 1995, he had these recollections:

> "We actually knew a few days before V-E Day that the war was ending. So, when it was announced in our office that V-E Day had actually come, it was no surprise. President Roosevelt, whom we always called The Boss, had died only the previous month. Our main reaction to V-E Day was that The Boss had known it was coming when he died. It would have been terrific if The Boss had lived to see V-E Day. But at least he had the satisfaction of knowing it was coming."
>
> —*World War II Secret Service agent Milton Lipson*

It was Winston Churchill who would give voice to the moment as he addressed a British crowd just after the announcement of Germany's surrender:

> "God bless you all. This is your victory! It is the victory of the cause of freedom in every land. In all our long history we have never seen a greater day than this. Everyone, man or woman, has done their best. Everyone has tried. Neither the long years, nor the dangers, nor the fierce attacks of the enemy, have in any way weakened the independent resolve of the British nation. God bless you all."
>
> —*Prime Minister Winston Churchill, May 8, 1945*

President Harry Truman, still quite new to his job, announced V-E Day in a 9 A.M. radio broadcast, setting off wild celebrations across the United States.

Mary Heena was working as a "Rosie the Riveter" at Grumman Aircraft Engineering Company when she heard the news, and her life was changed in an instant:

> "Feelings were great. Everybody was cheering and hollering. My husband, Edward, was serving in the Pacific, and I was praying for him to come home safe—which he did. I worked on the F-6 and F-7 planes—riveting, putting in rudder rods and putting on hoods. But, after V-E Day, I never worked another day at Grumman. I turned in my tools and badge that day."
>
> —*aircraft factory worker Mary Heena*

V-E Day marked the end of nearly three-and-a-half years of deadly combat, of devotion to duty, of pain and sacrifice by American men and women in Europe and at home. For Europeans, it brought the sweet winds of peace after 5 years, 8 months, and 8 days of ugly warfare.

Only one Axis menace remained: Japan.

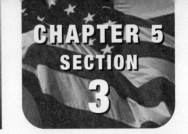

Victory in the Pacific

The Fall of Japan

On August 6, 1945, 28-year-old Lieutenant Colonel Paul Tibbets lifted his B-29 off the island of Tinian, 1,500 miles south of Japan. He commanded a mission that would change the history of air combat . . . the history of warfare . . . truly, the history of the world.

Just over 40 years had passed since another historic takeoff, at Kitty Hawk, North Carolina, where the Wright Brothers launched the infancy of air flight. Orville and Wilbur could never have imagined what their feat would set in motion: from World War I dogfights to the creation of the most powerful U.S. combat air force; from the Mighty Eighth to Tibbets's six-and-one-half hour flight to Japan, carrying the world's most destructive weapon ever: the atomic bomb.

The American Dilemma

The Japan that the American air forces targeted was still the bristling war machine that had carved much of Asia into a sprawling, ruthlessly held empire. From mid-May to mid-June, the Army Air Forces struck major industrial sites in Japan, dropping leaflets beforehand warning civilians to flee. Industries in six major cities were bombed into dust. The United States also had carried out a fire-bombing campaign, during which the AAF lost less than two percent of their B-29 bombers. The month of raids had made about 100,000 people homeless. By July, in preparation for the planned ground invasion, a naval blockade and continued bombing had cut off food and other supplies and left Japan devastated.

American strategists had planned two separate invasions for Japan's major islands, one in November 1945, and another in March 1946. The battle for the heart of Japan was expected to be very costly: President Truman had been told to expect 250,000 to 1 million U.S. casualties, and an equal number of Japanese casualties.

In July 1945, the Allies called on Japan to surrender unconditionally. But fanatical Japanese warmakers had not yet been humbled. With a remaining 2-million-man army and fleet of warplanes, Japan defiantly rejected the demand.

The Allies now faced the daunting task of taking Japan island by island, city by city. This was the specter that Truman faced when he decided to resort to a weapon with destructive power the Japanese could not have dreamed of: the atomic bomb.

Making a Bombing Plan

While scientists and engineers worked on creating a powerful bomb to bring an end to the war, the military launched a program to determine how to transport, arm, and detonate the bomb over Japan. The man chosen to head this ultra-secret project was Lieutenant Colonel Paul Tibbets.

Tibbets had enjoyed a rising career in the Mighty Eighth. In the summer of 1942, he headed a bomber squadron that flew their B-17s to England for further training and combat. In August, Tibbets flew his bomber, the *Butcher Shop*, to lead the historic mission to Rouen—the first American daylight bombing raid by B-17 heavy bombers.

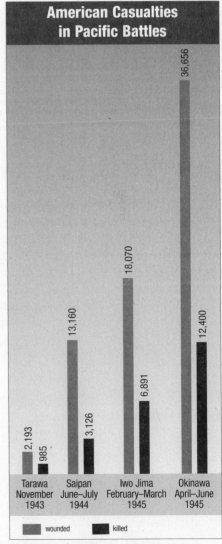

American casualties rose sharply as the battle lines moved closer to the Japanese home islands.

Because of his flying skills, Tibbets later was chosen to ferry top generals to secret meetings on the African front. His passengers included General Dwight D. Eisenhower.

Tibbets, one of the most experienced combat bomber pilots in the Army Air Forces, was called to Colorado Springs in September 1944 to organize a bombardment group to deliver the atomic bomb.

"Silverplate"

Tibbets wasted no time in putting together a team, the 509th Composite Group. Using the code name "Silverplate," he had a virtually unlimited access to resources, which he used to bring together 15 B-29s and 1,800 men. The team chose the remote base at Wendover, Utah for their training.

The operation, known as "Mission 13," would involve three weather/reconnaissance aircraft to check out four possible bombing targets in Japan: the cities of Hiroshima, Kokura, Niigata, and Nagasaki. Tibbets himself, with a hand-picked crew from the Mighty Eighth, would have the awesome task of dropping the bomb. They would be accompanied by six other planes: a backup bomber, a photo plane, a flying scientific laboratory to measure the blast, and the three reconnaissance planes. Bombing would be visual in clear weather for maximum accuracy and subsequent evaluation.

Science Link   Splitting the Atom

The bomb got its unlikely start as theories scribbled in pencil on old envelopes in the hands of Albert Einstein. Einstein's theories prompted Italian physicist Enrico Fermi to perform tests in which he bombarded radioactive atoms with atomic particles to release small amounts of energy.

Einstein, a German Jew, moved to America in 1933, after Hitler's rise to power. The Danish scientist Neils Bohr visited Einstein in 1939, giving him the news that European scientists had split a uranium atom, producing a small release of energy. This process is called "fission". Bohr predicted that the release of neutrons from fissioned atoms could be made to initiate a chain reaction. The power released by this chain reaction could reach undreamed-of proportions. Under special conditions, a very fast chain reaction might produce an enormous release of energy that could be harnessed to make a weapon of immense power.

By the time war had broken out in Europe, these theories had been proven in laboratory tests. At the urging of his colleagues at Princeton University, Einstein wrote President Roosevelt, warning him that the Germans might build such a weapon. Roosevelt quickly ordered the creation of an extraordinary project—code named the Manhattan Project—to develop an atomic bomb.

Einstein himself did not participate in building the bomb. At the center of the enterprise was a brilliant group of United States, British, and refugee scientists. While engaged in wars in Europe and the Pacific, the United States summoned the manpower and resources to complete in just four years a project that otherwise might have taken half a century. The cost would total about $20 billion in today's dollars.

The project had its share of delays, and it became clear that by the time the new weapon was ready, Germany would be defeated. The target changed, from Germany to Japan.

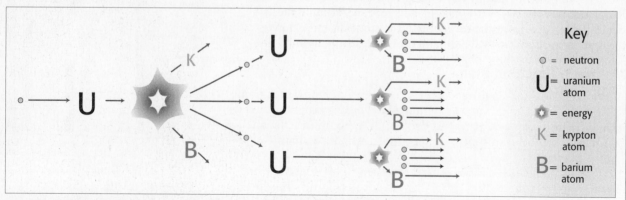

Key
○ = neutron
U = uranium atom
✦ = energy
K = krypton atom
B = barium atom

One neutron strikes the nucleus of a uranium atom, which releases energy and two or more neutrons to sustain a chain reaction. Krypton and Barium are only two of the many possible by-products of the reaction.

Mission 13 would originate at the American airbase on Tinian, one of the Mariana Islands. Tinian was the nearest spot from which heavy bombers could reach mainland Japan. The airbase had 8,500-foot runways, among the longest in the world at that time and able to accommodate the heavy B-29s.

The "Superfortress"

Tibbets himself, along with his crew, would have the weighty task of dropping the bomb. They would fly a new B-29 Superfortress named *Enola Gay*, after Tibbets's mother. The B-29 was the first aircraft to boast fully pressurized crew compartments, finally ending the problems of regulating oxygen and temperature. It carried a system that allowed one gunner to fire five pairs of machine guns. It had a pneumatic bomb bay door and tricycle landing gear. The B-29 was larger and faster, flew higher and farther, and carried a bomb load more than twice that of the B-17.

As big and fortified as it was, the Superfortress could not withstand the shockwave of an atomic bomb. From the moment the bomb left the bomb bay until it detonated at an altitude of about 1,900 feet, Tibbets would have to get eight miles away or be blown to bits by the blast. The *Enola Gay* would be flying at an altitude of six miles over Japan. How would it gain the extra two miles? Tibbets determined that he could execute a quick, diving 155-degree turn in the opposite direction. This maneuver would take the aircraft over ten miles away by the time the shock wave from the explosion would reach the aircraft. Tibbets recalls, "The plane shook, and I yelled 'Flak', thinking a heavy gun battery had found us." After a second, lighter shock wave hit them, Tibbets knew they would survive.

Most of the six-and-one-half-hour flight to Japan would be spent over water. The crew had to figure out how to quickly orient themselves once they reached land. They practiced by flying off the waters of the Caribbean and over Cuba, then moved to their departure site in the Pacific in May 1945.

Testing the Bomb

The first test of an atomic bomb took place on July 16, 1945, in the "Trinity" test near Alamogordo, New Mexico. The observers wore eye protection from the burst of light, which was expected to be as intense as 10 suns. There was a flash, and then a shockwave that shook observers, even at a great distance. The explosion sent a mushroom cloud shooting up 40,000 feet in the air. Searing heat at the detonation site melted desert sand into glass.

The man who had supervised the actual building of the bomb, J. Robert Oppenheimer, was both thrilled and troubled by what he experienced. A force of nature like none other had been unleashed; the sheer magnitude and power of it overwhelmed the mind.

Two types of bombs emerged from the Manhattan Project: one fueled by uranium and the other by plutonium. Tibbets would drop a uranium bomb, nicknamed "Little Boy." It was more slender and longer (12 feet) than the plutonium version, "Fat Man."

Little Boy contained an explosive power equal to 20,000 tons of TNT and would do the damage of about 2,000 conventional bombers.

A mushroom cloud rises into the air after the atomic bomb is dropped on Nagasaki.

Inset: Nuclear physicist Julius Robert Oppenheimer (left) with Major General Leslie Groves (right) study the remains of the tower from which an atomic test bomb was detonated near Alamogordo, New Mexico.

The Bombing of Hiroshima

Lieutenant Colonel Paul Tibbets and the Enola Gay

Not until the night before the mission did officials brief the *Enola Gay* crew on the revolutionary nature of the bomb they would carry and its unimaginable destructive force. It had been a worrisome night: Four B-29s had crashed and burned on Tinian's runways. Crashes were not unusual there, so the team had decided not to activate the bomb until they were safely in the air.

On Sunday morning, August 6, the crew prepared to fly. Once activated, the bomb could not be deactivated. The plane itself could not descend and land for any reason, because the bomb was set to detonate at an altitude of about 1,900 feet, triggered by an atmospheric pressure sensor. Mission 13 had all the features of a science-fiction movie. But it was real.

A little after 2:30 A.M., the *Enola Gay* rolled down the runway and lifted off the ground safely. The event was set into motion. Three hours after takeoff, at dawn, the plane and its escorts flew over Iwo Jima, the battle site that had claimed tens of thousands of lives. It was a reminder of the reason President Truman had sent them on this mission: to bring the Japanese to their senses and save millions of lives.

At 7:30 A.M. the atomic bomb was activated.

At 8:30 A.M. the reconnaissance aircraft identified the clearest of the four sites: Hiroshima.

At 9:15 A.M. they dropped the bomb.

He executed his drop-and-reverse maneuver. They were flying away from the blast, which pursued them at 1,100 feet per second as the mushroom cloud rose nine miles into the sky.

All the planes escaped the blast. They left behind an incinerated city, seen in aerial photographs taken afterward. These photographs showed destruction unlike anything ever seen. The center of Hiroshima had been vaporized, except for the skeletons of three concrete buildings. An estimated 60,000 people died. More than 100,000 people were injured, most of them burned by the radiation. Some 200,000 people were left homeless.

The United States ordered Japan to surrender or face a second atomic bombing. Astonishingly, the horror did not change the minds of the Japanese war council. Many people thought the descriptions of the blast to be exaggerated. No communications came from Hiroshima, causing skeptical leaders to disbelieve the super-bomb explanation. The scene was simply too awful to imagine.

Ready to fight to the death, Japan refused to surrender.

This second mission would deliver a "Fat Man" plutonium weapon, a descendant of the bomb tested at Alamogordo, New Mexico. It was supposed to be dropped on Kokura, Japan, on August 11; however, the date was moved to August 9 in hopes of encountering better weather.

The plane, named *Bock's Car*, was another B-29 Superfortress. The mission encountered very bad weather. The crew spent an agonizing 10 minutes over the target city as clouds prevented visual contact. Finally, a secondary target city had to be selected.

That was how the city of Nagasaki entered the history books.

Over Nagasaki, the crew flew back and forth twice, using up precious fuel, without finding a break in the cloud cover. On the third run, however, they found a clear spot. The bomb was released. It was 11:02 A.M. local time. The results were spectacularly and catastrophically similar to those at Hiroshima. The blast that hammered the city destroyed more than half of the buildings. An estimated 70,000 people died.

Victory over Japan

Incredibly, even after the destruction of Nagasaki, the war council split, 3 to 3, on whether to give up. For the first time in the war, the military men asked Emperor Hirohito to vote. The weary leader voted for peace. The one Japanese request that the Americans granted was to keep the Emperor on the throne. The United States agreed, and made the Emperor subject only to the Supreme Commander of Japan, which would be General Douglas MacArthur.

On August 14, 2,000 planes of the AAF carried out one final bombing of Japan, which was still at war. As B-29s were returning from the mission, President Truman announced the unconditional surrender of Japan. America and its allies rejoiced.

Surrender

As in Europe, the B-29s in Asia stayed on after the surrender to ferry food and medical goods to prisoner of war camps. Although American POWs suffered under German control, Japanese camps were far worse. The conditions were so harsh that of the 5,400 or so AAF prisoners in Japanese camps, only about half survived, whereas the survival rate of AAF prisoners in German camps was about 99 percent.

What had begun as a sneak attack on ships at rest at Pearl Harbor nearly four years earlier ended on the deck of a ship with the flourish of a pen. On September 2, 1945, aboard the battleship U.S.S. *Missouri,* Japanese officials signed the formal surrender agreement. General MacArthur officially received the surrender from the Japanese.

Thus, in two flashes of horror, the most deadly and most costly war in the history of the world came to an abrupt conclusion.

Personal Impact

Most Americans agreed with President Truman's decision to use atomic weapons on Japan. They were weary of war, and recognized that Truman's decision saved countless lives, Japanese and American. After V-E Day, the men in the Eighth Air Force found their joy had turned to deep concern for their future. Some of them would go back to the States to finish up their military service. A smaller number would remain in Europe. Other war-weary

A ship bearing American servicemen arrives into San Francisco harbor.

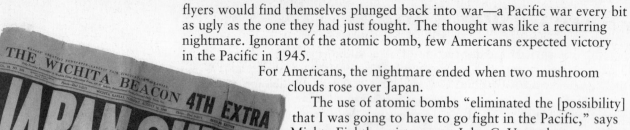

flyers would find themselves plunged back into war—a Pacific war every bit as ugly as the one they had just fought. The thought was like a recurring nightmare. Ignorant of the atomic bomb, few Americans expected victory in the Pacific in 1945.

For Americans, the nightmare ended when two mushroom clouds rose over Japan.

The use of atomic bombs "eliminated the [possibility] that I was going to have to go fight in the Pacific," says Mighty Eighth waist gunner John C. Veenschoten. "Whatever device was used to end the war and save lives, in my opinion, was the best thing that could have happened."

America Rejoices

Headlines like those on the left leaped from the front pages of newspapers across America. "Peace!" was the news on the radio, on street corners, at the grocery store. Since V-E Day, Americans had held their breath, waiting for the day when they could exhale and truly celebrate the end of World War II. Finally, the boys were coming home.

As always in war, the gleefulness of victory was tinged with solemnity in remembrance of victory's awful cost. In an address declaring September 2 to be V-J Day, President Harry Truman echoed the full range of human emotions on the occasion. His radio address, heard live aboard the U.S.S. *Missouri* as part of the surrender ceremonies, was also heard across America.

"The thoughts and hopes of all America—indeed of all the civilized world—are centered tonight on the battleship *Missouri*. There on that small piece of American soil anchored in Tokyo Harbor, the Japanese have just officially laid down their arms. They have signed terms of unconditional surrender.

"Four years ago, the thoughts and fears of the whole civilized world were centered on another piece of American soil—Pearl Harbor. The mighty threat to civilization which began there is now laid at rest. It was a long road to Tokyo—and a bloody one.

"We shall not forget Pearl Harbor.

"The Japanese militarists will not forget the U.S.S. *Missouri*. . . .

"Our first thoughts, of course—thoughts of gratefulness and deep obligation—go out to those of our loved ones who have been killed or maimed in this terrible war. On land and sea and in the air, American men and women have given their lives so that this day of ultimate victory might come and assure the survival of a civilized world. . . .

"We think of all the millions of men and women in our armed forces and merchant marine all over the world who, after years of sacrifice and hardship and peril, have been spared by Providence from harm.

"We think of all the men and women and children who during these years have carried on at home, in lonesomeness and anxiety and fear.

"Our thoughts go out to the millions of American workers and businessmen, to our farmers and miners—to all those who have built up this country's fighting strength, and who have shipped to our Allies the means to resist and overcome the enemy.

"We think of our departed gallant leader, Franklin D. Roosevelt, defender of democracy, architect of world peace and cooperation. . . .

"Now let us set aside V-J Day as one of renewed consecration to the principles which have made us the strongest nation on earth and which, in this war, we have striven so mightily to preserve."

—*President Harry Truman, radio address, September 1, 1945 (September 2 in Japan)*

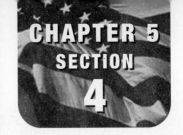

Remembering

The Costs of War

War statistics—the cold, hard numbers—cannot measure the courage and endurance of the men and women who brought down dictators and restored peace to nearly half the world. Yet numbers can show us the "big picture" and teach us the costs of war.

> **Americans in World War II.** More than 16 million Americans served in uniform during World War II. Of these, 292,131 died in combat and 115,185 died of other causes. 671,846 other Americans were wounded.

Gathering accurate statistics during the chaos of World War II was extremely difficult. On the ground, whole armies were captured or scattered during battle. Mass movements of fleeing or homeless civilians remade the population distribution of many countries. Historians cannot say how many people died as a result of warfare, disease, starvation, or execution, but the number is at least 30 million, and possibly 50 million. Losses in the countries where the greatest numbers lost their lives—the Soviet Union and China—are impossible to verify.

American and British war totals are the most reliable. The Army Air Forces, and the Eighth Air Force in particular, kept careful records of men and aircraft lost. This ultimate sacrifice can be measured. Historian Stephen A. Ambrose compiled these disturbing statistics:

> "For those in combat, the risks were higher in the AAF than in the American ground forces. In total, the AAF, about one third of the U.S. Army, took about one ninth the battle casualties of the entire Army, but most AAF men were mechanics or command and staff officers, staying on the bases in England that were relatively safe, especially as opposed to the foxholes of infantry soldiers. But the AAF had a far higher proportion of officers in action than did the Army as a whole—including fighter pilots, about half of all flying personnel were officers—and twice as many AAF officers died in battle than in all the rest of the Army. On average, almost 4 percent of the bomber force were killed or missing in action on each mission. . . ."
>
> —*Stephen E. Ambrose,* The Wild Blue:
> The Men and Boys Who Flew the B-24s Over Germany

One of the remarkable facts about the men of the Mighty Eighth was that most of them knew, each time they climbed into their planes, what their chances were of coming back uninjured. The statistics were gloomy.

The Mighty Eighth made a mighty sacrifice in Europe. Typically, there are more wounded than killed in war. Here the numbers are reversed, a chilling detail that speaks about the dangers of air combat.

Reflections and Tributes

Stories of the Mighty Eighth will be told for generations. They are stories of exceptional courage, patriotism, and determination. Some of those stories end in great sadness, but others extend long beyond the war, when the pilots, gunners, navigators, mechanics, and medics returned to do other great deeds at home.

The dream of Generals Hap Arnold, Carl Spaatz, Ira Eaker, Jimmy Doolittle, and many other AAF leaders became true in 1947, when the United States Air Force (USAF)—an independent

> **The Mighty Eighth in War.** 350,000 Americans served in the Eighth Air Force during World War II. Sixty percent, or 210,000 Americans, served as airmen. 26,000 lost their lives in action, and 28,000 became prisoners of war.

wing of the armed forces—was born. A number of Mighty Eighth veterans made significant contributions to the new Air Force as it reached ever higher into the skies, and even into space.

Continuing to Serve

Eighth Air Force flying ace Chuck Yeager earned his status the hard way. He downed his first enemy plane on his seventh mission in Europe and his next "kill" on his eighth outing. It was an ill-fated No. 8, though,—Yeager was shot down, and crash landed in Nazi-occupied France. There he was rescued by the French Resistance, one of many underground units secretly fighting to win their countries' freedom. Resistance fighters saved countless airmen from going to the German POW camps and ushered them safely back to England.

AAF policies barred downed airmen from returning to air combat. But Yeager had only tasted battle, and he wasn't ready to quit. The bold pilot appealed personally to General Eisenhower to let him fly again. Yeager soon returned to the cockpit, shooting down nine more German fighters and becoming a double ace by the war's end.

His service to his country did not end with the Nazi surrender. Yeager became a test pilot with the new USAF, helping to develop America's own experimental jet aircraft. Yeager won fame in 1947, when he became the first pilot ever to fly faster than the speed of sound, breaking the sound barrier. In 1953, at the controls of a machine that was more rocket than airplane, he set a new world speed record: an astounding 1,650 miles an hour.

> *"Germany lost the war the day it started. Your bombers destroyed German production, and Allied production made the defeat of Germany certain."*
>
> *—Hjalmar Schacht, German Finance Minister*

German Airmen and Leaders Pay Tribute

What difference did the Eighth Air Force make in the outcome of the war in Europe? Ask the experts: the defeated members of the German Luftwaffe. After the war, often from prison cells, German airmen spoke openly and knowledgeably about the Allied victory in the skies.

Many former Nazi officials, including the condemned Luftwaffe chief, Herman Goering, agreed that strategic, daytime bombing was a huge success. Some believed the bombings won the war, and that the war could have been won by airpower alone, without a ground invasion.

The genius of the bombing strategy, they asserted, came in the bombing of oil fields and rail yards. Germany's oil supplies remained adequate until the spring of 1944, when the Eighth Air Force proceeded to unload some 70,000 tons of bombs on oil refineries. A year later, oil supplies had been bled dry; lack of fuel grounded planes and halted production lines. Major General Albrecht von Massow of the Luftwaffe said, "The attack on German oil production in 1944 was the largest factor of all in reducing Germany's war potential."

Whatever Germany did manage to produce, it could not transport. The Mighty Eighth targeted roads, bridges, railroad yards, and numerous other transportation facilities, dropping a third of its bombs, about 235,000 tons, on railroad yards alone. Field Marshal Albert Kesselring of the German Army said simply, "Allied air power was the greatest single reason for the German defeat."

Honoring the Eighth

In 1995, the 50th anniversary of the end of World War II, the Air Force chief of staff, General Ronald R. Fogleman, accepted an invitation to speak to a reunion of Mighty Eighth members. Above the din of many speeches and ceremonies that year, Fogleman's tribute rings loud and true:

> "You [the Eighth] stepped forward from all walks of American life at a time when this country needed you. You came forward to defend America against the forces of tyranny and evil. . . . From the humble beginnings in August 17, 1942, when Ira Eaker first led 12 B-17s on a heavy bombing mission against the marshaling [railroad] yards at Rouen, France, you built the Eighth Air Force into a massive air armada that devastated the Nazi warmaking machine.

> "Some 200,000 people—40 bomb groups, 15 fighter groups, two photo reconnaissance groups. For us today, it is mind boggling to think about the logistics, the organization and the training involved in such an effort. . . . [Y]ou made it work. You made it happen. . . .

> "You were faced with nearly impossible odds in those early days. No capability for long-range fighter escort; statistically impossible to complete a tour of duty; but you and your fellow airmen, you all persevered. You would not be denied, and you established another legacy for us: You established the enviable record of never, never being turned back by enemy action. . . .

> "By the close of the war, the Mighty Eighth had struck where no other forces could go in enemy-held territory. You had either damaged or destroyed 19,000 German fighters, and within your ranks, you could boast of 261 recognized aces and 14 Medal of Honor winners. . . .

> "In the end, your courageous performance during World War II led to the birth of today's United States Air Force in September 1947."

> —*speech by General Ronald R. Fogleman,*
> *United States Air Force chief of staff,*
> *to the Eighth Air Force Historical Society Reunion Banquet,*
> *Sept. 9, 1995, to honor the 50th anniversary of World War II*

Looking Back With Pride

On the 60th anniversary of the Mighty Eighth, in January 2002, veterans shared their innermost thoughts about the war and their role in it.

"I always felt we were fighting a worthwhile war," says Mighty Eighth gunner John C. Veenschoten. "I was there for a reason. And we were so encouraged by everyone in America about what we were doing. It was an important era. A wonderful time. That's one of the reasons that we were so loyal to it. . .

"That American flag meant *everything*."

Mighty Eighth veteran B-17 co-pilot Craig Harris sums up the effort this way:

"We were trying to stop the killing. The way to stop the killing was to stop the war. The way to stop the war was to win it. Every time we struck a target and struck it well, we felt we had made a step in that direction. Every time we dropped our bombs in open fields or woods . . . we felt like that was a day wasted and we got shot at for nothing. . . .

"Most of the guys took it very seriously; they did it with a lot of pride and a lot of conviction that we were doing the right thing."

Harris conveys the views of many members of the Mighty Eighth:

"I wouldn't want to do it again for anything. But I wouldn't let you take it away from me for anything. I'm glad I did it, and when I look back on it, the fellowship of the flyers, the professionalism they exhibited, and the pride, and the camaraderie, the memories are priceless.

"It was a good war, if there is such a thing."

Should the air forces become an independent branch of the military?

As you have read, military aviation was first seen as a natural extension of the army. The Army Air Service in World War I helped the Army by observing enemy movements, dropping bombs during battles, and engaging in mid-air dogfights with other fighter planes. The navy also experimented with airplanes. Both the army and navy hoped to optimize their performance on land and at sea with the support of air power.

In the 1920s and 1930s, many airmen pushed for an independent air force separate from the navy and army. With no war to fight, they could not prove their case on the battlefield. Committees studied the issue in 1924–1925 and again ten years later. Both times, the government concluded that the Army Air Corps should remain part of the army. The Morrow Board remarked in 1925, "the next war may well start in the air, but in all probability will wind up, as the last one did, in the mud."

Another disadvantage for those seeking an independent air force was the government's reluctance to spend much money on defense. In 1935, the Army included only 165,000 enlisted men, down from millions in 1918. There was little enthusiasm for creating a new military organization with its own expenses.

Circumstances changed with the start of World War II. The AAF proved beyond a shadow of a doubt that strategic and tactical bombing missions could play a key role in the war effort. While tactical bombing was carried out with the close cooperation of the Army, strategic bombing raids over Germany had little interaction with the Army and involved an entirely different set of challenges.

By 1945, the Army Air Forces had grown much larger than the Army Air Service of World War I, with many more planes and crew members in the air and on the ground. The grand size and scope of the Army Air Forces supported the argument that they had come of age and were ready for independence.

The use of the first atomic bombs on Hiroshima and Nagasaki ushered in the Atomic Age, with significant changes to the United States' defense policy.

The nuclear arsenal became the key-stone of American defense by discouraging potential enemies from starting a war. Airplanes were the only logical delivery system of this new weapon in the 1940s and 1950s, because rockets were still too primitive to carry bombs long distances. In World War II, rockets had seen use only in the final months, as the Germans lobbed explosives at Britain from bases in Europe. The Army Air Forces and the Navy both developed airplanes with the nuclear option in mind.

After the war, the Cold War drove American leaders to reorganize the armed forces into one governmental department. The Army favored unification of the armed forces and was willing to give the Army Air Forces their independence under this framework. The Navy objected to the plan. Navy officials feared that the Navy would lose its independence. They were particularly concerned that an independent Air Force would take the place of the Navy's own aviation program.

The USAF participated in the conflict in Korea.

The Navy finally agreed to unify if the authority of the new organization was limited and the Navy could include "such aviation as may be organic therein." The National Security Act of 1947 was passed on July 26, placing the Army, Navy, and the brand-new Air Force on an equal footing under one organization which would eventually become the Department of Defense. Thirty years after American pilots joined the dogfights over the Western Front, and five years after the Eighth's first strategic bombing missions over France, the Army's airmen had won their independence.

Making a Decision

Use the following steps below to evaluate the decision to create an independent United States Air Force. As you read each step, think of the important issues raised by the debate over giving the air forces their independence.

◆ **Identify the problem and express it clearly.** First, determine whether a decision is needed; then clarify what needs to be decided. What is the issue you want to resolve or the goal you want to achieve? Describe the two opposing viewpoints in this debate in your own words.

◆ **Gather Information.** Find out facts about the issue. Be sure that your sources are reliable. List two facts and one opinion for each side in this debate.

◆ **Identify options.** Be sure to consider all the ways an issue might be handled. Stating the options clearly will help you decide. Describe the options faced by the United States in this debate.

◆ **Predict consequences.** Identify the pros and cons of each choice. List one advantange and one disadvantage of each option.

◆ **Make a decision.** Evaluate your options; choose the one with the most acceptable consequences. Describe the choice made by the United States government and explain why this was considered the best choice.

Additional Resources

To learn more about the Eighth Air Force and World War II, the Eighth Air Force Historical Society recommends the following books:

- Freeman, Roger A. *The Mighty Eighth*. Motorbooks International, 1991.

- Freeman, Roger A. *The Mighty Eighth War Diary*. Motorbooks International, 1990.

- Freeman, Roger A. *The Mighty Eighth War Manual*. Motorbooks International, 1991.

- Freeman, Roger A. *The Mighty Eighth in Color*. Specialty Press, Inc., 1992.

- Gurney, Gene. *The War in the Air: A Pictorial History of World War II Air Forces in Combat*. Bonanza Books, 1959.

- Miller, Donald L. and Henry Steele Commager. *The Story of World War II*. Simon & Schuster, 2001.

- Morrison, Wilbur H. *Fortress Without A Roof: The Allied Bombing of the Third Reich*. St. Martin's Press, 1982.

- Neillands, Robin. *The Bomber War: The Allied Air Offensive Against Nazi Germany*. Overlook Press, 2001.

- Werrell, Kenneth P. *Blankets of Fire: U.S. Bombers over Japan During World War II*. Washington: Smithsonian Institution Press, 1996.

Answer Key

Page 11
Science Link

Question: What technological advantages does the airplane have over the dirigible?
Answer: The airplane is less explosive, safer, faster, more navigable, and carries more passengers.

Page 13

Question: Why did dogfights have a limited impact on the course of the war?
Answer: Airplane warfare was seen as having limited usefulness compared with airplane reconnaissance. In World War I, the decisive battles were still fought on land and at sea.

Page 17

Question: Why did the bombing of Guernica alarm people outside of Spain?
Answer: It warned other nations about the power of aircraft to destroy cities.

Page 19
Science Link

Question: What advantage(s) did radar give Britain during German attacks?
Answer: Radar gave Britain warning of incoming enemy planes; the signals detected the size, shape, and path of objects.

Page 21

Question: What were two possible reasons why London was a tempting target for the Luftwaffe?
Answer: London was within German fighter range for bomber protection, close to Europe, and capital of and biggest city in Britain.

Page 24

Question: Why do you think Japan felt confident in attacking these American bases?
Answer: Bases in Guam, Wake Island, and the Philippines were too far from mainland United States to be reinforced after the attack began. The Japanese attacked early on a Sunday morning, when many people were away from their posts.

Page 26
Literature Link

Questions: Why do FDR and Takamura urge their fellow citizens not to forget Pearl Harbor? How does each writer express confidence?
Answer: FDR wanted Americans to remember the Japanese aggression and the danger it posed, in order to rally the country to war. Takamura wanted Japanese to celebrate their victory, both as Japanese and as Asians, over "the Anglo-Saxon powers." Both appeal to citizens' national pride and their conviction in the superiority of their religious beliefs.

Page 28

Question: How were war bonds good for Americans and good for the war effort?
Answer: They encouraged people to save and earned them interest; it raised money to fund the war.

Page 29

Answers will vary.

Page 32
Diversity in the Military

Question: What reasoning might have led military authorities to limit the participation of minorities in combat, and what reasoning caused the authorities to change their minds?
Answer: Authorities suspected that Japanese and Japanese Americans might be disloyal or even be spies. Other minorities were already kept segregated in parts of the country and thought to be inferior; some military men did not want to serve with them. As the need for troops became acute, leaders reluctantly drafted minorities, who served with distinction.

Page 41

Question: How is nylon an example of science influencing history?
Answer: Nylon greatly aided the war because it could be put to so many uses. As a fabric, it made stronger parachutes and tents; in other forms it could be used to make, ropes, cords, and airplane tires.

Page 48

Question: Why did bombing accuracy decrease when planes flew at high altitudes?

Answer: From high altitude, the bomb has to travel farther to reach the target. The longer the fall, the more aiming errors are magnified, and the greater the influence of variations in aircraft speed and wind drift. "Trail," or the distance by which the bomb lags behind the bomber's position at bomb impact, is greater and more variable.

Page 49

Question: What were two reasons why Rouen was chosen as a target in July 1942 instead of a city in Germany?

Answer: Rouen, under Nazi occupation, was a major transportation center for routing troops and supplies. It was a short distance from Britain, and U.S. warplanes could not yet reach Germany without unacceptable losses.

Page 50

Question: Why was the oxygen mask necessary?

Answer: The aircraft cabins were unpressurized and the atmosphere at high altitudes lacked oxygen. A crewman could die quickly if his oxygen supply were cut off.

Page 53

Question: How do you think changes in temperature, wind speed, or cloud cover affected the operation of U.S. bombers and fighters over Europe?

Answer: Cold temperatures could cause ice on the planes and cause guns and other machinery to freeze up. A strong tailwind could help by pushing the planes along; a strong headwind could slow the flight, using more fuel and endangering the return flight. Cloud cover made takeoffs and landings difficult and prevented the crews from seeing oncoming enemy aircraft and the target sites.

Page 55

Answer: about one-half

Page 63
Science Link

Question: Why are reconnaissance photographers often referred to as the "unrecognized heroes" of World War II?

Answer: Although they were not well-known, they faced a high risk of being shot down and provided critical information and assessment, such as damage done to target sites.

Page 72

Question: Why were briefings important?

Answer: Briefings provided crews with all the information they needed in order to carry out a mission successfully.

Page 82

Question: What do these maps indicate about Allied progress in those two weeks?

Answer: The Allies broke out of their beachhead at Normandy and advanced across western France.

Page 96

Question: Why didn't the Eighth Air Force need aircraft carriers?

Answer: While the Pacific War was fought over large expanses of ocean, the Eighth was able to hit its targets from land bases in England, and later, in liberated France.

Page 99

Question: Why did the planes have to land in China?

Answer: The aircraft carried enough fuel to reach Japan from the aircraft carrier, but not enough to guarantee a return to the same spot. China was the nearest land in which friendly territory might be found.

Acknowledgments

Cover Design

Studio Montage

Interior Design

Prentice Hall (Paul Gagnon, Phyllis Hawkes) and Studio Montage

Photography

Cover: Corbis. **pp. iv–ix** Vivid Details, Copyright 1994. **p. 10** Getty Images/Hulton Archives.
p. 11 Getty Images/Hulton Archives. **p. 12** Getty Images/Hulton Archives. **p. 13** (top) National
Archives and Records Administration, (bottom) Corbis. **p. 15** Getty Images/ Hulton Archives.
p. 16 Getty Images/ Taxi. **p. 18** DK Picture Library. **p. 20** (top) DK Picture Library, (bottom)
Library of Congress. **p. 22** Getty Images/ Hulton Archives. **p. 23** Corbis. **p. 24** Digital Stock, Inc.
p. 25 The Mighty Eighth Air Force Heritage Museum. **p. 28** The Mighty Eighth Air Force
Heritage Museum. **p. 31** The Mighty Eighth Air Force Heritage Museum. **p. 32** Getty Images/
Hulton Archives. **p. 32** The Mighty Eighth Air Force Heritage Museum. **p. 33** The Mighty Eighth
Air Force Heritage Museum. **p. 34** The Mighty Eighth Air Force Heritage Museum. **p. 36** Franklin
D. Roosevelt Library. **p. 37** DK Picture Library. **p. 38** The Mighty Eighth Air Force Heritage
Museum. **p. 39** The Mighty Eighth Air Force Heritage Museum. **p. 40** The Mighty Eighth Air
Force Heritage Museum, (background) Vivid Details, Copyright 1994. **p. 41** Getty Images/ Hulton
Archives. **p. 42** Getty Images/ Hulton Archives. **p. 43** Getty Images/ The Image Bank. **p. 44** The
Mighty Eighth Air Force Heritage Museum. **p. 45** The Mighty Eighth Air Force Heritage Museum.
p. 47 Getty Images/ Hulton Archives. **p. 48** The Mighty Eighth Air Force Heritage Museum.
p. 50 The Mighty Eighth Air Force Heritage Museum. **p. 51** The Mighty Eighth Air Force
Heritage Museum. **p. 52** The Mighty Eighth Air Force Heritage Museum. **p. 56** The Mighty
Eighth Air Force Heritage Museum. **p. 57** The Mighty Eighth Air Force Heritage Museum.
p. 58 Getty Images/ Hulton Archives. **p. 59** (top, bottom) The Mighty Eighth Air Force Heritage
Museum. **p. 62** Getty Images/ Hulton Archives. **p. 63** The Mighty Eighth Air Force Heritage
Museum. **p. 64** The Mighty Eighth Air Force Heritage Museum. **p. 65** The Mighty Eighth Air
Force Heritage Museum. **p. 66** The Mighty Eighth Air Force Heritage Museum. **p. 67** The Mighty
Eighth Air Force Heritage Museum. **p. 68** Getty Images/ Hulton Archives. **p. 69** The Mighty
Eighth Air Force Heritage Museum. **p. 70** Getty Images/ Hulton Archives. **p. 72** (inset, background) The Mighty Eighth Air Force Heritage Museum. **p. 73** Getty Images/ Hulton Archives.
p. 75 The Mighty Eighth Air Force Heritage Museum. **p. 76** The Mighty Eighth Air Force
Heritage Museum. **p. 77** The Mighty Eighth Air Force Heritage Museum. **p. 80** Getty Images/
Hulton Archives. **p. 82** The Mighty Eighth Air Force Heritage Museum, Carter Collection.
p. 83 The Mighty Eighth Air Force Heritage Museum, Carter Collection. **p. 84** The Mighty Eighth
Air Force Heritage Museum. **p. 86** The Mighty Eighth Air Force Heritage Museum. **p. 87** Getty
Images/ Hulton Archives. **p. 89** The Mighty Eighth Air Force Heritage Museum. **p. 90** The Mighty
Eighth Air Force Heritage Museum. **p. 91** The Mighty Eighth Air Force Heritage Museum.
p. 92 Getty Images/ Hulton Archives. **p. 93** (inset) Getty Images/ Hulton Archives, (background)
Digital Stock, Inc. **p. 95** Getty Images/ Hulton Archives. **p. 96** Getty Images/ Hulton Archives.
p. 102 Getty Images/ Hulton Archives. **p. 103** The Mighty Eighth Air Force Heritage Museum.
p. 106 Getty Images/ Hulton Archives. **p. 107** Getty Images/ Hulton Archives. **p. 108** The Mighty
Eighth Air Force Heritage Museum. **p. 111** (inset, background) Getty Images/ Hulton Archives.
p. 112 Corbis/Bettmann Collection. **p. 113** Getty Images/ Hulton Archives. **p. 114** The Mighty
Eighth Air Force Heritage Museum. **p. 119** Getty Images/ Hulton Archives. **p. 120** Vivid Details,
Copyright 1994.

Maps

pp. 17, 21, 24, 27, 30, 35, 49, 55, 61, 78, 81, 97, 99, 104 Margaret Halliburton

Graphs/Illustrations

pp. 26, 27, 29, 54, 60, 74, 100, 109, 110 Studio Montage

Staff Credits

Joyce Barisano, Sandy Graff, Salena Hastings, Phyllis Hawkes, Tim Jones, Dotti Marshall, Jim
O'Neill, Luess Sampson-Lizotte, Amit Shah, Carol Signorino, Mark Staloff, Susan Swan

Epilogue

In the immediate post-World War II period the Army Air Forces began to reorganize in preparation to becoming a separate service apart from the U.S. Army. Three major commands were formed, the Air Defense Command (ADC), which would have the responsibility of defending the nation from external attack using fighter interceptors, the Tactical Air Command (TAC), which would have responsibility for all tactical fighter operations, and the Strategic Air Command (SAC), which would have responsibility for bomber and tanker operations and perform the nation's primary nuclear deterrent role. Later SAC would also assume responsibility for the nation's nuclear-armed intercontinental ballistic missiles as a key element of the mission of deterrence.

In March 1946 the Eighth Air Force was assigned to the newly formed Strategic Air Command headquartered at Andrews Air Force Base (AFB), Maryland, and later at Offutt AFB, Nebraska. The Mighty Eighth would serve as one of SAC's numbered Air Forces until SAC was deactivated on June 1, 1992. In those 46 years, men and women, and units of the Eighth Air Force would serve in the Cold War, the Korean War, the Vietnam War, Operation JUST CAUSE in Panama, and Operation DESERT SHIELD-DESERT STORM in the Persian Gulf War. Eighth Air Force responsibilities included strategic bombing missions with B-47, B-52 and FB-111 jet bombers, aerial refueling missions using the KC-97 powered by reciprocating engines, and KC-135 and KC-10 jet tankers as well as high altitude reconnaissance missions flown by U-2 and TR-1 aircraft. During the Cold War, the Mighty Eighth also operated Titan and Minuteman land-based intercontinental ballistic missiles in SAC's deterrent posture. Perhaps one of the most noteworthy combat operations conducted by the Eighth Air Force was the Linebacker II mission of December 1972, when B-52s bombed military targets in Hanoi and Haiphong, North Vietnam. This effective bombing operation convinced the North Vietnamese to return to the peace negotiations in Paris, France, bringing the war to a close. In the intervening years the headquarters of the Eighth would be located at several Air Force Bases including: Carswell AFB, Texas; Colorado Springs, Colorado; Westover AFB, Massachusetts; Andersen AFB, Guam; and finally in its current location at Barksdale AFB, Louisiana. Personnel of the Mighty Eighth served with distinction in all of these conflicts and hundreds of combat crew members would pay the supreme sacrifice of losing their lives while flying training and combat missions.

Since June of 1992 the Mighty Eighth has been assigned to Air Combat Command (ACC) headquartered at Langley AFB, Virginia. While assigned to ACC the Eighth participated in the Kosovo Air Campaign in the Balkans and the War on Terrorism beginning with air operations in Afghanistan. Jet bombers like the B-52, the B-1B and now the B-2 Stealth Bomber continue to carry war to the enemies of the United States and its Allies. More importantly the men and women of the Mighty Eighth continue to serve with distinction in the high tradition of the veterans of World War II. Our nation is well served to have this distinguished war-fighting organization in its military arsenal.